Black Phoenix

History and Operations

of the

Marina Repubblicana 1943-1945

A German six engined Bv 222 flying boat ferrying a SMA attack craft to its target. A 1944 Decima MAS plan to ferry a unit in these aircraft to attack Suez was rejected in favor of a German-only mission using Marder. The German plan never materialized. (Drawing by Franco Harrauer)

Black Phoenix

History and Operations of the Marina Repubblicana 1943-1945

Vincent P. O'Hara

Enrico Cernuschi

Propeller Press

Propeller Press
631 E J Street
Chula Vista, CA
619-980-6170

Copyright 2014 by Vincent P. O'Hara and Enrico Cernuschi

All rights reserved. No part of this book may be reproduced or utilized in any form or by any means, electronic or mechanical, including photocopying and recording, or by any information storage and retrieval system, without permission in writing from the publisher.

ISBN: 978-0615978611

Printed in the United States of America

Table of Contents

Preface	2
Chapter 1. The Frame	5
Chapter 2. A Troubled Partnership	9
Chapter 3. A Square Deal................................	16
Chapter 4. Before the Republic	24
Chapter 5. Anzio and Nettuno.........................	31
Chapter 6. Elba and Provence.........................	45
Chapter 7. The Ligurian Sea	52
Chapter 8. The Adriatic 1944-1945	62
Chapter 9. Dragon's Teeth..............................	70
Chapter 10. A Forgotten War...........................	74
Appendix I. Organization of the Marina Repubblicana	78
Appendix II. Warships and Auxiliaries of the Marina Repubblicana	81
Appendix III. Surface Actions fought by Marina Repubblicana Units....................	98
Bibliography..	100

Acknowledgements

This book covers a subject that has received superficial and often inaccurate coverage in the English language. and the authors would like to acknowledge the help of some special people in writing this history.

The late Aldo Fraccaroli, founder of the school of Italian naval enthusiasts, participated in the 1945-46 commission investigating former Regia Marina personnel who had joined the Marina Repubblicana. A stubborn royalist he demonstrated understanding during those hard times and preserved in the decades since the same regard for justice and balance, thereby giving witnesses to the spirit of those chronologically-recent, but poorly understood times.

By mere chance Federico Peyrani, of the Libreria Militare book store in Milan, was able to connect the authors with Fabio Cordini, whose father was an Antisom sailor, and who generously supplied a series of never published photos which enrich this book.

The late Sergio Nesi, from Bologna, by far the most important author writing on the subject of the Decima MAS and who was himself an attack craft pilot who served off Anzio, in the Provence, and in the Adriatic Sea.

Lorenzo Scardovi, formidable uncle of Enrico Cernuschi and a CB midget submarine veteran between 1943 and 1945 whose serenity brightens the mood of this essay.

Erminio Bagnasco, the leading Italian naval historian who generously allowed us to use many illustrations from his excellent magazine Storia Militare that he founded twenty years ago and still directs. As an old MTB commander he spent many hours trying to explain to the authors the technical difficulties and tactics of the small fast boats he loves so much.

The famous naval architect Franco Harrauer, who is currently building a flotilla of commercial catamarans on the Amazon River, contributed many fine drawings that delight the eye and give a ready appreciation of how the small craft that fill these pages matched up against one another.

Last but foremost, the authors wish to acknowledge their spouses and families. Vincent O'Hara thanks his wife, Maria and his children Yunuen and Vincent. Enrico Cernuschi thanks his wife, Piera and daughter, Arianna.

Preface

On 9 September 1943 American and British forces landed on the Italian mainland south of Naples at Salerno. This invasion followed secret and hasty negotiations between the Allies and Marshal Pietro Badoglio, Italy's prime minister since the deposition of Benito Mussolini, and the supreme command's chief of staff, General Vittorio Ambrosio. So far as the Allied military negotiators understood, Rome had agreed to sign an armistice and join the war against Germany. Badoglio, however, preferred a neat exit from the conflict with as little harm to his nation as possible.

Unfortunately events did not unfold the way either party wanted. The Allies compelled Italy's negotiator to sign the agreement they desired according to their schedule. However, when Badoglio learned, literally hours before the event, that troops were coming ashore earlier, in less strength, and further south than expected, he tried to defer announcement of his deal with the Allies, and even considered reneging. It was far too late. Operating under a veil of secrecy forced by the need to hide the negotiations from their German partners, most of Italy's political and military leaders learned of the armistice when Badoglio announced it on Radio Rome the evening before the Salerno landings. The result was a disaster for the Italian government and high command that, compounded by poor leadership, led to the collapse of Italy's army and air force.

Notwithstanding the secrecy surrounding the armistice negotiations Berlin was ready for an Italian attempt to "betray" Teutonic interests ever since Mussolini's arrest on 25 July 1943 and it acted swiftly and effectively. By the end of October German forces had contained the Allied army just north of Naples and occupied most of the peninsula. German commandos rescued Mussolini, Hitler's good friend, from captivity and ushered him north where, under the Fuhrer's patronage, he established the *Repubblica Sociale Italiana*--a supposedly independent state allied to the Reich. The German high command preferred an outright occupation under a military government over the restoration of an Italian puppet state and resisted, with much success, the establishment of independent Italian institutions and authority. During the rest of the war 217,991 Italians died, nearly as many as the 226,532 who lost their lives before the armistice. This included 158,195 in the fighting against the Germans, the Allies, and with each other and another 59,796, nearly all civilian, in bombing attacks.[1]

Between October 1943 and April 1945 there existed two Italian navies. The first was the Regia Marina, which signed an agreement on 23 September to cooperate with the Allies and then became a co-belligerent fighting on the side of the United Nations after the Kingdom of Italy declared war on Germany on 13 October. The second navy was the Marina Repubblicana. This was a much smaller force unofficially born immediately after the armistice when certain Italian naval units fought alongside the Germans in the Adriatic and Aegean as the result of local agreements or coercion. In one case a complete unit, the Decima Flottiglia MAS, elected to join the Germans while individual officers and men made the same choice due to a sense of honor or a feeling that they had been betrayed by their government. After the 23 September foundation of Mussolini's Repubblica Sociale Italiana the Marina Repubblicana became an official service of that government although it always fought under German command and relied upon the Reich for weapons and supplies.

Histories of the war have had little to say about the Marina Repubblicana especially since the events in which it participated were often judged to have small relevance to the war's outcome. Only recently have the German naval campaigns fought in the Mediterranean after the Italian armistice been appreciated as critical to the Reich's larger strategic goal of engaging the Allies as far as possible from its vital interests.

Black Phoenix provides a comprehensive account of the Marina Repubblicana's operations while summarizing the conditions that led to its establishment and its role within the larger Axis war effort. This history has been difficult to construct for several reasons. Many Allied reports of the period assumed that all naval units they faced were German. Italian records have often misidentified targets and both sides have overstated results. Many German and Italian records of the period have disappeared. Nonetheless, it is possible to establish that the Marina Repubblicana was instrumental in the surprising success of Germany's maritime guerrilla war along the coasts of the

---

[1] The number of civilians killed prior to the armistice was 22,186. *Morti e dispersi per cause belliche negli anni 1940-1945*. Rome: Istituto Nazionale di Statistica, 1957.

Mediterranean from September 1943 to May 1945 earning in the process the trust of its suspicious allies and the respect of its foes.

Chapter 1. The Frame

The war Italy fought between 1940 and 1943 was characterized by a failure to understand the conflict's true nature. Mussolini, Italy's economic elite, and most of the population believed the nation was engaged in a sort of Medieval tournament rather than a fight for survival and that whatever the war's outcome Italy's economic and continental power status within the so-called *Mediterraneo allargato* (greater Mediterranean), from Tangiers to the Indian Ocean, would survive.

The joy most citizens displayed when the armistice with the Allies was announced on 8 September 1943 was rooted in the misperception that the warring states would respect Italian integrity in a sort of replay of Vichy France's 1940-1942 situation and in the belief that the war would soon be over anyway as Germany would be quickly defeated without Italy as a partner.

On 9 September came the hard awakening and with it a severe national shock. The armistice was not the dawn of a spreading European truce; instead it rendered the entire peninsula a battleground. Within two days the Germans had ruthlessly seized control of most of the country and even threatened the success of the main Anglo-American landing at Salerno. Italy's king and supreme command fled Rome in haste relocating to Brindisi in the far south and leaving the nation's army and air force facing an impossible situation with inadequate leadership. Within a few days most of these services had crumbled except for the fascist militia units that had already joined the Germans, and a few scattered formations whose commanders independently made the same choice.

This disaster made the decision to ask the Allies for terms seem a debatable choice. The reconstruction of the Italian fascist party followed from 9 September until the liberation of Mussolini three days later and the institution, on 23 September, of the new *Repubblica Sociale Italiana*, which formally restored the Axis alliance, at least in name. The reality, of course, was that Mussolini's government had almost no independent existence beyond Berlin's convenience.

In the German perspective the Italian armistice was a good bargain. The Reich captured a huge stock of weapons and material. Italy's 3 million man army--a third of them in Italy without weapons or even steel helmets--no longer weighted on the Axis economy. After the summer 1943 crisis Berlin dispatched fourteen divisions to Italy--a fraction of the 179 German divisions deployed on the Eastern Front--while German forces in the Balkans and Southern France remained constant from 25 July 1943 until the final retreat more than a year later. German manpower diverted to Italy was balanced by the progressive entry into the Reich's labor force of 450,000 Italian prisoners of war and 140,000 Italian civilian workers. This allowed the Germans to call to arms by April 1944 a new class of their citizens and facilitated a restoration of Wehrmacht strength on the Eastern Front.

1. *A MAS (*Motoscafo Anti Sommergibili*) motor torpedo-boat (MTB), an SMA (*Motoscafo Silurante Modificato Allargato*), the final version of the small boats designed to force enemy harbors and used, since 1942, as tiny MTBs), an MTM explosive boat (*Motoscafo Turismo Modificato*) and a MTL (*Motoscafo Turismo Lento, slow motor boat) carrying a manned SSB type torpedo like the one used in the attempt to force Leghorn in December 1944. (Drawing by Franco Harrauer)*

The replacement of the *Regio Esercito* with more motivated (and German trained) units of the fascist republic hardly altered Italian front line strength. Before the armistice logistics allowed the deployment of one Italian army (the

6th), formed by four regular and six coastal divisions and other scattered troops in Sicily in July-August 1943; and the 7th Army with a similar strength (an average total of 220,000 troops) in southern Italy in September 1943. The fascist republican troops that participated increasingly from December 1943 in the campaign against the Allies evolved from brigade level formations to five divisions, including one formed by two brigade groups of

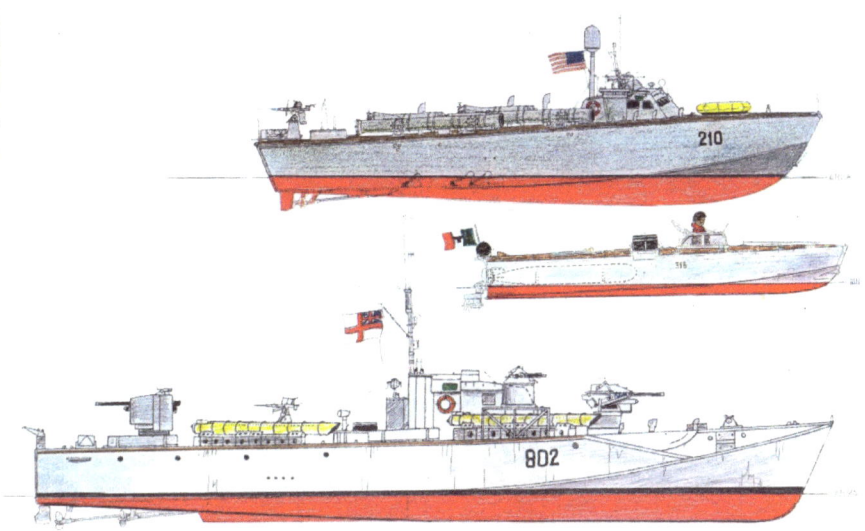

2. *A U.S. Navy PT boat of the Higgins 78 foot Type, an Italian SMA, and a British Fairmile D class motor gunboat. (Drawing by Franco Harrauer)*

Prince Junio Valerio Borghese's Decima MAS naval infantry. By January 1944 a further 178,000 Italian men (half fighting troops, half auxiliaries) served with the Wehrmacht in the Balkans, France, Russia and Germany. A year later the number stood at 165,000 men--more than half in Germany serving as flak personnel.

The situation was similar with the Italian air force. On 8 September 1943 the Regia Aeronautica, victim of a moral crisis and increasingly reduced efficiency, had only 129 modern fighters, about a third of them in service. The *Aeronautica Nazionale Repubblicana* (ANR) fascist republican air force deployed from January 1944, an average of ninety modern fighters flown by volunteers whose training had been upgraded by the Luftwaffe, with a constant 66 percent service rate until late April 1945. The ANR also deployed a torpedo bomber group from March 1944 until the spring of 1945 and two transport groups on the Russian front.

The German divisions in Italy were supplied with munitions and supplies from local resources and industries (these last quickly converted to the manufacture of German weapons and spare parts, including airframes, engines, V1, and V2 components) with a constant output of munitions and spare parts, until April 1945, similar to 1940-1943 production rates while the military balance in Italy remained constant with a very favorable (for Germany) ratio of one Axis soldier to three Allied.

The German strategy conceived since September 1942 was to gain time and space in the Mediterranean theatre pinning down the greatest possible enemy force with the purpose of winning the war, by now compromised along all the fronts, with a great strategic victory in the West (during the pending, future invasion or, better, well inside the continent and far from the coasts). In fact, this vision was realized in December 1944 (and proven bankrupt) when the Wehrmacht concentrated an army twice the size of its Allied adversaries at the Battle of the Bulge.

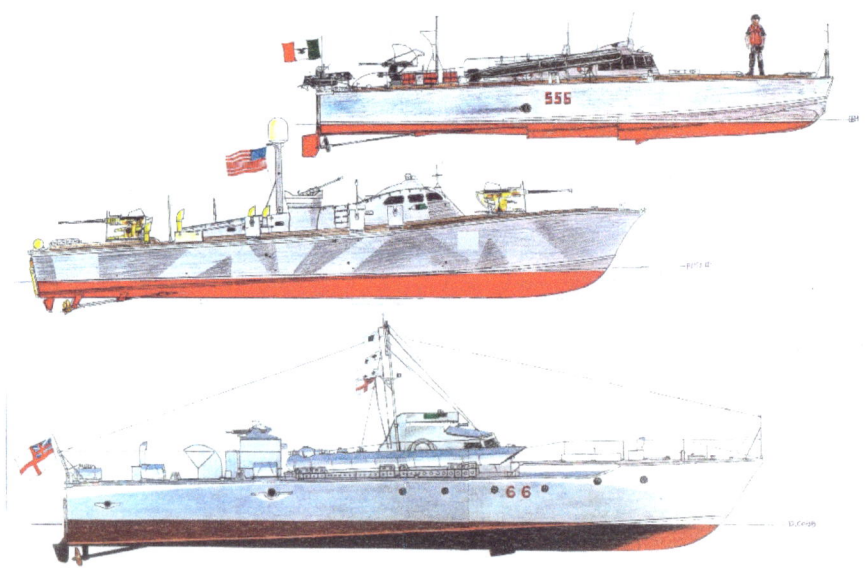

3. *A Marina Repubblicana MAS boat, a USN PT of the ELCO 70 foot type, and a British Vosper 70 foot MTB. (Drawing by Franco Harrauer)*

Chapter 2. A Troubled Partnership

The full story of the frustrations the German navy suffered with its allies during the two world wars is worthy of a book in itself. An overview is relevant to this study because of the background it provides for understanding how the creation of the Marina Repubblica, imperfectly realized a longstanding ambition of the Kriegsmarine and how any true cooperative relationship was compromised before it even began.

In its swift evolution from a coastal defense force to worldwide power, the German navy tended to consider itself the senior partner in every alliance it entered. This attitude, favored by its many technological accomplishments, allowed the Kaiser's Imperial Navy to control directly, with little regard for form and diplomacy, the Turkish and Bulgarian fleets. The Kriegsmarine reprised this performance in 1941 with the Romanian, Bulgarian, and Croatian navies. However, when major partners were involved, like Austria-Hungary in 1914-1918 and Italy in 1940-1943, matters did not go all Germany's way.

When the First World War erupted Berlin proposed to Vienna with great insistence many bold naval enterprises like landings in Albania and Greece, the dispatch of its battle fleet to Constantinople, attacks on the French squadron patrolling the entrance to the Adriatic Sea, and cruiser raids in the Mediterranean. Vienna brushed these suggestions aside and the Germans were compelled to limit themselves to harsh private criticisms of their Hapsburg ally masked by a correct outward demeanor.

The situation was similar twenty years later with Italy. Notwithstanding the huge size disparity between the treaty-constrained German fleet and the Regia Marina, Berlin's contemptuous opinion of Italian staff, personnel, ships, and doctrine dominated during the 1920s and 30s. Operational contacts between the two navies, excluding some limited cooperation in Spanish waters between December 1936 and March 1939, did not begin until June 1939 when the commander in chiefs of the Kriegsmarine and Regia Marina held a cautious meeting at Friederichshaven. That encounter proved of little consequence and the situation hardly improved over the next twelve months. The Germans declined to address many sensitive questions asked by the Italians about radar, electric torpedoes, high capacity batteries, fast diesel engines, magnetic mines, or large motor torpedo boat (MTB) designs. Rome,

4. In July 1943 Germany planned to revolutionize submarine warfare in the Mediterranean by assembling thirty Type XXIII Elektroboote at Toulon. This program began in October 1943 and expanded with thirty more at Genoa and fifteen units ordered at Monfalcone in February 1944. This photo shows a pair of Elektroboote sections at the Genoa Ansaldo Sestri yard in 1944. None were completed and by April 1945 the Germans were shipping the sections previously sent to Italy back to Germany. Another 1944 program to assemble at Monfalcone twenty-nine Type XXVII Seehund midget submarines was cancelled. (Storia Militare)

in turn, did not meet any of the Reich's requests to support its auxiliary cruisers, submarines, and blockade breaking activities.

This lack of cooperation, notwithstanding a formal correctness by both sides, continued after Rome's declaration of war on 10 June 1940. That same day, for example, the Seekriegsleitung (SKL) Diary reported an order by the Kriegsmarine's Grossadmiral Erich Raeder, to give the new ally some technologic help in the fields of electric torpedoes, radar, and sonar.[2] The next morning, however, conditioned reflexes resurfaced inducing

---

[2] *Kriegstagebuch*, part A, Vol. 10, 11.06.1940, 118-19.

Kriegsmarine staff to delete any reference to the torpedoes and to reveal only the existence of a land-based radar prototype the Italians determined, three days later, to be similar to their own "RDT 3" experimental metric set already activated at Livorno. It was only after the Matapan defeat that the Regia Marina learned of the existence of the Kriegsmarine's seaborne radar sets and, more importantly, about those of the British. Not until that summer did Germany sell Italy a dozen sonars while the first (and, until December 1942, only) Kriegsmarine radar set reached an Italian warship in April 1942.

On the other hand, the Regia Marina staff resisted German interference in their naval operations from the first day of their common war. The Kriegsmarine's June 1940 attempt to influence the Italian navy with the freshly promoted Vice Admiral Eberhard Weichold and his tiny staff of six men (ignoring the detail that Weichold had begun a crash course in Italian only a week before) revealed the Kriegmarine's superior attitude toward its new ally. From the beginning Weicholdt's reports to Grand Admiral Eric Raeder, the Kriegsmarine's commander in chief, were rich in poison. The difference between these documents and his honey-filled conversations with Italian admirals and officers illustrate the gap between Germany's intentions and desire for an effective liaison with the Regia Marina.

The contemporary and theoretically identical activities of the less verbose Italian Admiral Giotto Maraghini, attached to the Kriegsmarine staff in Berlin in 1940-1941, had little impact and naval collaboration between the Axis partners remained limited to minor matters like the Regia Marina's submarine campaign in the Atlantic Ocean, and the passage of blockade runners.

Faced with an increasing need for fuel and other German aid, Supermarina, the Italian navy high command, finally admitted Weichold to its situation room in February 1941, but only as an observer. On 1 August 1941, after he had begun championing (with little effect) Italian requests for more oil and improved air support, the German admiral become a full member of Supermarina with the right to participate in its debates. Admiral Maraghini, replaced in June 1941 by Rear Admiral Giuseppe Bertoldi, an enthusiastic advocate of the Italo-German partnership, received the same progressive rights in Berlin. Nonetheless, the Italians always had to politely limit their advice with almost no real effect on German operations while Weichold at once began to tell the Regia Marina's deputy chief of staff, Admiral Luigi Sansonetti, what he needed to do. Weichold's ideas included attacking the radar-equipped British battle fleet at night with the few modern destroyers available, or ferrying supplies to North Africa in cruisers and destroyers, or conducting shore bombardments in Libya with battleships, or raiding enemy traffic with the battle fleet unhindered by short-ranged destroyers, or deploying all available submarines as "secure" transport to Libya, and so forth. In some cases, like using warships or minelaying submarines to ferry small and sometimes decisive cargos to Libya, Weichold's idea had already been planned. The reaction to his less practical input was, at best, a polite "Hear, hear." There simply was not the oil, the destroyers, and the air reconnaissance required for top priority escorts duties and the risky and non-productive raids the Germans considered the sinews of sea power.

In early January 1941 Admiral Raeder asked Hitler for permission to assume direct control of Italy's navy, a proposal the Chancellor refused, knowing well the fragility of Mussolini's political position at the time. On 6 June 1941 Raeder again pressed Hitler in a memorandum that stated the Italian navy's officer corps and sailors (but not its admirals) had made good efforts during the last few months and that with German leadership, planning, and discipline much more would be possible.[3]

Once again Hitler disregarded this suggestion although in July the British received information about the project and concluded that the Regia Marina was by now under German control.[4] A renewed endeavor undertaken on 2 December 1941, this time supported by Hitler himself, to put the Italian navy at the direct orders of the newly created *Oberbefehlshauber Süd* (OBS) and Marshal Alfred Kesselring, was immediately dismissed by the Italian general chief of staff, General Ugo Cavallero. Nonetheless, the increasing number of the German coastal warships and submarines in the Mediterranean necessitated an increase in Weichold's staff to 344 men by January 1942. A contemporary project by the Kriegsmarine, the so-called Reiniche study, to pair, as in Turkey during the previous world war, German commanders with Italian ones at all levels of command and at sea, paying off the two battleships and the cruiser at Brest to acquire the personnel for such a task, was soon shelved.

---

[3] Lagevortraege des Oberbefehlshaber, 258-262.
[4] Santoni, "Doveva consegnarsi," 93.

After September 1942 Sansonetti noted a new "respectful and disciplined" attitude in Weichold. The reasons for the German admiral's apparent about face were uncertain but it showed in his reports to Raeder who began to think about a replacement. On 26 February 1943 Weichold sharply rebutted a request from SKL that he later characterized as unrealistic. "I deeply concur with the Italian navy's opinion that it is using all its forces to deliver the decisive supplies to the Tunisian front and that it is right in stating that its planning and direction of the operations must not be jeopardized by extemporary requests from the Army Command in Africa . . ." Less than six days later he was sacked and replaced by Admiral Wilhelm Meendsen-Bohlken.[5]

Raeder himself resigned on 30 January 1942 after a series of operational failures culminating in the December 1942 Battle of the Barents Sea. His successor, Grand Admiral Karl Dönitz, who was more abrupt than his old-style predecessor, was already pursuing his version of the German dream of controlling the Italian Navy. First, in February he dispatched Vice Admiral Friedrich Ruge, formerly responsible for escorts and minesweeping along the French Atlantic coast, to train Supermarina on how to conduct convoys. The real purpose was to lay the groundwork for a single, unified escort command under German leadership. Next, on 14 March during his first visit to Rome, Dönitz petitioned Mussolini directly to create a parallel German command structure for the Regia Marina. Admiral Arturo Riccardi, the Regia Marina's chief of staff refused in front of his startled dictator. As a result, Ruge's command was confirmed on 24 March as a consultative position under Supermarina and the situation evolved in a positive way from the Italian point of view as Ruge proved to be a reasonable man and good comrade, unlike the arrogant and aggressive Meendsen-Bohlken. By 17 May Riccardi was able to win Meendsem-Bohlken's replacement with Ruge who had accepted by the end of April Supermarina's appreciation that the naval and air situation in the Sicilian narrows was totally different from conditions in the English Channel.

---

[5] Weichold, "Il contributo della Marina germanica," 25.

5. *A Decima MAS recruiting poster (Enrico Cernuschi)*

Dönitz traveled to Rome on 12 May 1943 looking to improve his strained relationship with Riccardi but the journey was unproductive and a final confrontation between the Kriegsmarine and the Regia Marina seemed in the offing. On 13 July Dönitz declared to Hitler that he was ready to personally take command of the Italian navy adding, on the 17th, that it was necessary to swiftly seize the Regia Marina's battle fleet and its main bases. Along these lines the German admiral was planning, with the blessing of the OKW's General Alfred Jodl, a subtle coup. The idea, which originated in early 1943, was to replace the Italian monarch Victor Emmanuel III, with his son, Prince Umberto, considered more favorable towards the Reich, or at least more malleable. Mussolini would become the country's sole ruler and the nominal commander of Axis forces in the Mediterranean, which would, navy included, actually be led by a German staff.

This plot included Umberto's cousin (and third in the line of succession), Admiral Aimone, Duke of Aosta, from early 1943. The liaison with the Duke was Commander Junio Valerio Borghese. According to Dönitz's plan a young Italian admiral acceptable to the battling nucleus of the officer corps would lead the reformed Regia Marina, with the help of a German staff. The names considered included Rear Admiral Giuseppe Manfredi, who had a tough-guy reputation from his time commanding North-African harbors in 1941-43, Admiral Antonio Legnani, the submarine force commander since December 1941, and the Berlin-based Admiral Giuseppe Bertoldi.

Mussolini's fall did not alter this program, beyond the removal of Ruge, considered too chummy with the Italians, and the return, on 12 August, of Meendsen-Bohlken, a choice which promised nothing good to Rome. The situation grew more tense when Hitler twice refused to meet with King Victor. The monarch, Prime Minister Badoglio, and Comando Supremo chief of staff, General Ambrosio thus saw their hopes for a commonsense compromise conclusion of the war in the East or a separate, Vichy-style armistice vanishing.[6]

The Wehrmacht forced by surprise the Brenner Pass fortifications on the night of 30 July, stunning and scaring the Italian generals in Rome and completed its dispositions in northern Italy by 6 August. Marshal Rommel was to instigate the planned crisis by presenting an ultimatum to King Victor Emmanuel. On 4 September the field marshal made a diary entry that, "I am to have an audience of the king shortly." Nonetheless Hitler, despite the pleas of his generals to act swiftly, hesitated out of concern for Mussolini, imprisoned by the new regime in a secret location.

On 7 September, fearing such a coup, King Victor ordered the Regia Marina's new chief of staff, Admiral Raffaele de Courten, to replace admirals Duke of Aosta at Spezia and Duke of Ancona at Venice and send them to Rome. Aimone of Aosta was embarked forcibly on 9 September 1943 on the torpedo boat *Indomito*. Ancona was bundled onto a floatplane on 11 September and rushed south to Brindisi. Already, on the evening of 8 September, Marshal Badoglio had reluctantly picked up the microphone and announced an armistice with the Allies. The final German attempt to hijack the Regia Marina had been too late.

---

[6] See Festorazzi, "Führer, liquidiamo il capitolo Russia."

Chapter 3. A Square Deal

Early in the morning of 9 September 1943 the Italian battle fleet sailed from Spezia and Genoa following Supermarina's orders issued in response to the Armistice. Until he heard Badoglio's broadcast, the fleet commander, Admiral Carlo Bergamini, was unaware of the pending armistice and he had been expecting to sortie against the Allied forces landing at Salerno. Instead, De Courten ordered him to head for Sardinia. Once at sea, however, the German capture of La Maddalena, the fleet's destination, and the destruction of Bergamini's flagship, the battleship *Roma* by two Luftwaffe delivered Fx-1400 airborne guided-bombs, forced the battleships, cruisers, and destroyers to make for Malta instead.

6. Admiral Antonio Legnani in September 1943. He was the Marina Repubblicana's first chief of staff, but died in an automobile accident in October 1943. (Storia Militare)

Even earlier that same morning, with gunfire echoing in the streets of Rome, Prime Minister Badoglio, King Victor, Chief of Staff Ambrosio and many of Comando Supremo's generals fled the capital, motoring across Italy in a car caravan along a route plotted to avoid German checkpoints. On the Adriatic coast they embarked on a Regia Marina corvette, which ferried them to the port of Brindisi in the south. Badoglio later wrote that the decision to flee the capital was made to prevent the Germans from establishing a new government that would repudiate the armistice.[7]

---

[7] Badoglio, *Italy at War*, 83-84." Others have been less generous in their interpretation of Badoglio's action. As one historian noted, "The documentation and literature on the surrender of Rome is extensive and as complicated as that in the United States about the responsibility for failure to anticipate the Japanese

Germany considered the armistice and the Italian navy's adherence to the king's orders an act of treachery and some vicious fighting at sea and around bases in Italy and the Balkans followed over the next few weeks. But the Kriegsmarine was also practical. It realized from the first day after the armistice that it lacked the personnel to man not only the small warships it seized, or found on the slips in Italy and elsewhere, but also to maintain in service the naval bases and yards, not to mention the merchant vessels, depots, and communication networks of central and northern Italy. In fact the plans already discussed to take control of the Italian navy had been dominated by this basic problem--a lack of personnel. As there was no alternative, the Kriegsmarine once more had to assume the mask of the friendly comrade asking for collaboration with Supermarina on the afternoon of 11 September 1943. This request came less than 24 hours after the signature of a truce in Rome between the Germans and a group of Italian ministers led by the elderly and highly influential Marshal Enrico Caviglia, a World War I hero who enjoyed a status in Italy similar to that held by Marshal Phillipe Pétain in France.

7. *Commander Borghese's official portrait. (Sergio Nesi)*

---

attack on Pearl Harbor. See O'Reilly, *Forgotten Battles*, 65.

8. *A Marina Repubblicana recruiting poster from late 1943. "Honor. Sailors! Gather for the salvation of the fatherland!" (Enrico Cernuschi)*

The secrecy of the armistice process followed by the prime minister and king's abrupt flight south fostered confusion and disunity amongst the government members and military commands still in Rome. The Italian navy staff knew of Badoglio's efforts to delay the broadcast of the armistice, and this seemed to confirm their worst fears, already advanced by the army minister, General Antonio Sorice late on the afternoon of 8 September that Badoglio had first deceived and then kidnapped the king. In the days following Sorice attended every government meeting repeating this opinion to all.[8] Many naval officers came to the same conclusion and given this environment, it was little surprise that on 12 September Supermarina staff gave the German request for collaboration a favorable hearing.

The mood of the Italian admirals was already soured by a BBC broadcast made on 11 September. In this transmission the British exploited an opportunity to score propaganda points with home and global audiences and characterized the gathering of the Italian battle fleet at Malta as an ignominious surrender. The inconvenient truth, that no ship had hauled down its flag, that the Allies were courting Italian co-belligerency, and that Italian sailors were dying in combat with the now common enemy of the United

---

[8] Bragadin, "Ho visto il messaggio del Re a Caviglia." Monelli, *Roma 1943*, 101-7.

Nations and Italian Kingdom, were ignored. This and subsequent reports from Allied media fueled the lingering suspicion of many Italians that the Allies had employed deception to obtain a cheap victory over Italy and were now throwing the country under the German bus.

Following negotiations with the Germans on the 12th, the retired Grand Admiral Thaon di Revel asked Senator Gaetano Scavonetti, the State Attorney, to draft a document outlining terms of collaboration with the Germans. Both men judged Scavonetti's final document "useful for the navy and respectful of the armistice terms."[9] There then followed a meeting in Thaon di Revel's house between the top Italian admirals present in Rome: the former chiefs of staff, admirals Domenico Cavagnari and Arturo Riccardi, the former battle fleet commander Angelo Iachino, the deputy chief of staff Luigi Sansonetti, and the admiral appointed by Caviglia as commissary to the navy, Emilio Ferreri. They all agreed that the German proposal presented an opportunity. Cavagnari and Riccardi pointed to the precedent of the French navy which had collaborated with the Kriegsmarine in a series of noncombatant roles in order to preserve a presence in its various bases in occupied France and to guard its materials.

There were other currents active in Rome encouraging collaboration despite the king's decision to come to terms with the Allies. General Sorice's belief that the old monarch had been kidnapped by Marshal Badoglio was later repeated many times by Commander Borghese thus reconciling his declared loyalty to the royal house with plans to create a new monarchy with the Duke Aimone of Aosta or his son Amedeo, born on 27 September 1943, as sovereign.[10]

In this drama, however, Borghese was nothing more than a fringe player and the Grand Admiral Thaon di Revel, president of the Senate since 27 July 1943 was the actual kingmaker. His role on 12 September and after, until Mussolini suppressed the Senate on 28 September 1943, was critical, granting

---

[9] ACS, "L'8 settembre 1943 al Ministero della Marina."

[10] The German army, particularly the Abwher, supported this program until 26 July 1944, when Himmler sent the 10 month old duke and his mother, Irene of Greece, to a concentration camp in Austria. Mussolini opposed this idea, even if he never completely dropped it in view of a possible re-unification of the country after the war.

9. A poster implying that members of the Decima MAS were popular with girls. From the first the Decima MAS enjoyed great success in its recruiting efforts. (Enrico Cernuschi)

as he did institutional legitimacy to the renewed Axis policy in Italy. Considering his huge prestige in the navy, it was natural that an increasing number of Regia Marina's officers in Rome begun to orientate themselves from 13 September "in an orthodox way", as the young diplomat, Luigi Bolla noted in his diary, "towards the Germans to save the Navy's honor."[11]

On 13 September, Admiral Sansonetti advised the navy ministry officers in Rome that the German navy's request for collaboration was being accepted. Everyone was free to follow their conscience adding that the Grand Admiral had stated that it was not possible to dictate each individual's choice in such a situation and that during the Risorgimento Italians had been obliged to choose opposite paths, but that both were legitimate if pursued with honesty and honor and that only history would be able to say which was the better one. He concluded saying the admirals Cavagnari, Riccardi, and Iachino, the three top ranking navy officers in Rome, had approved his words.[12] Sansonetti then shut down Supermarina and ultimately

---

[11] Bolla, *Perché a Salò*, 101-2.
[12] ACS, "L'8 settembre 1943 al Ministero della Marina" Thaon di Revel's allusion to the Risorgimento was meant to recall the vicissitudes of Admiral Francesco Caracciolo, the commander of the Neapolitan navy who, disenchanted by the Bourbon flight to Sicily after a brief and ruinous war against France, and the British scuttling of the Neapolitan fleet, joined Napoleon in February 1799. For four months he led the Partenopea Republic's frigates and gunboats against the British and his own king's warships. Made a prisoner after the republic's

made his own personal choice, undertaking on 25 September a strenuous and dangerous three week trek south to join the king and legal government. The agreement with the Germans was finally signed on 14 September.

As these events played out in Rome a local truce was negotiated at Spezia, on the morning of 9 September, between the base commander, Admiral Giotto Maraghini, and the Germans. Commander Borghese led the Decima MAS Special Forces unit based there. Borghese later insisted that the armistice caught him completely by surprise and that he waited several days for orders that never arrived, in the meanwhile easily repelling several German attempts to enter the Decima MAS barracks. Finally, on 12 September the local German command contacted him with an offer of collaboration. On 13 September, after releasing from his unit those who wished to leave, he signed a private agreement with the Kriegsmarine, in the style of a 16th century Condottiero. This allowed the Decima MAS to function as a unit under the Italian flag and his command. On 15 September Borghese encountered Marshal Caviglia, who had relinquished his role in Rome and was returning to his house in Liguria. Caviglia confirmed the commander's worst suspicions about Badoglio and Ambrosio and even spoke to Borghese's sailors saying: "Remember that from you and only from you will someday the glorious Italian navy rise again."[13] On 21 September Borghese traveled to Rome to meet Admiral Ferreri. The encounter was not a happy one. Borghese thought Ferreri was too diffident and, above all, wanted to rule "his navy" unit that, since 12 September, was growing in an impressive way as the fame it gained during the war was attracting thousands of recruits, army personnel included.[14]

The situation between Borghese and Ferreri cleared on 23 September with the institution of the new fascist republican government and the appointment of Admiral Antonio Legnani as navy secretary and chief of staff.[15]

---

surrender, he was hung from the yardarm of a Sicilian frigate and his body tossed into the sea. Caracciolo's memory was sacred in the Italian navy, which named four warships after him, and the fact that same story was repeating itself escaped no one.

[13] Bordogna, *Borghese e la X Flottiglia MAS*, 36.
[14] Bandini, *Vita e morte segreta*, 287.
[15] Legnani was reluctant to accept and asked Thaon di Revel's advice. The Grand

According to the postwar commission of inquiry created to judge the Regia Marina personnel's conduct following the 8 September armistice, 11 admirals, 37 captains, 74 commanders, 101 lieutenant commanders, 293 lieutenants, 220 sub-lieutenants, 142 midshipmen, 50 cadets, and more than 3.000 warrant officers, petty officers and boatswains also joined the Marina Repubblicana. This totaled 7.9 percent of the officers and 15 percent of the petty officers in the Regia Marina's ranks on 8 September 1943.

Borghese met Legnani on 21 September and the two men established a clear entente. Legnani would limit himself to commanding the navy's general infrastructure and to recovering from the Germans everything he could. Borghese would organize and lead the fast coastal forces and attack craft. The admiral, however, died in a car accident on 19 October, less than a month later and was replaced as Secretary by his right hand, Captain Ferruccio Ferrini, who had been wounded in the same crash while Admiral Giuseppe Sparzani, formerly captain of the battleship *Vittorio Veneto*, became chief of staff. The relationship between Ferrini and Borghese developed into a stormy one. The captain was a good sailor and submarine commander, but he wanted to lead the navy first and last and pursued the impossible dream of an almost full restoration of the Italian navy's previous condition.

On 9 January 1944 the prince's sailors at Spezia captured ("like a Tom Mix movie," according to the report) two of Ferrini's envoys sent there to assume command of the Decima MAS. On 13 January 1944 Ferrini engineered the arrest of Borghese in Mussolini's lobby at Gargnano, after the dictator agreed that Borghese was politically dangerous. The Maestrale naval infantry battalion immediately sortied from Spezia to free the commander by a march towards Salò that would have crossed the republic like a knife through butter. The resolution was the only one possible: Borghese was liberated on 25 January and Admiral Sparzani replaced Ferrini as secretary on 13 February while Borghese become deputy chief of staff definitely settling the chain of command.

Admiral told him to make the more difficult choice for the country's sake. Legnani thus took the post telling Mussolini that he would limit himself to recovering as much of the organization and ships as he could before passing his desk to someone else. From an interview of Emilio Legnani. See Gatti, *Il Tigullio*, 58-59.

The partnership with Sparzani proved excellent providing Borghese the complete support of the navy's land organization and allowing a common opposition to the many German attempts to assert absolute control over the remnants of the navy's infrastructure and authority. In the end Mussolini, always worried that Borghese's sailors were more loyal to their commander than to him, sacked Sparzani on 21 February 1945 replacing him as navy secretary with the army colonel, Bruno Gemelli who, despite warnings from the fascist party, soon fell under the spell of Borghese's charisma.

Chapter 4. Before the Republic

The post-armistice history of Italian-German naval cooperation at sea begins with orders given on 10 September by the Italian Northeastern, Yugoslavian, Albanian, and Greek commands. Lacking guidance from Rome these formations made on-the-spot agreements with their local German counterparts mostly to cooperate against Partisan threats to the Italian population and interests that arose during the armistice's chaotic aftermath. These agreements resulted in many of the small Italian naval craft along the Croatian coast coming under German control, always under the condition they would not be used against other Italian units. By 11 September these included:

10. *One of the small motor barges manned by Italian black-shirt from Zara that were armed with machine guns and used off the town with a couple of motorized fishing vessels in October 1943. (Editrice Militare Italiana)*

At Sebenico the old MAS (*motoscafi armati siluranti*) boats, *MAS 439*, *431*, and *433* of the 7th Squadron along with the auxiliary submarine chasers *AS 126* and *143*, and a half dozen motorboats and patrol craft.

At Zara the gunboat *Levrera*.

At Gravosa the small torpedo boat *T 7*.

At Durazzo the the old torpedo boats *Pilo* and *Missori*, the auxiliary cruiser *Arborea*, the auxiliary minesweepers *Di Lio*, *Nicola Padre*, and *San Giovanni*, and the Regia Guardia di Finanza (customs) patrol boat *Saba*.

At Valona the small escorts *Pola* and *Rovigno*.

Given that the Kriegsmarine had in the Adriatic just four hard-used MTBs divided between Pola and Venice, these Italian vessels--which sailed under the Italian flag and command, along with the armed steamers *Italia*, *Goffredo Mameli*, and *Marco*--proved invaluable to the Germans as they rapidly reasserted control of the coast between the Corfu Channel and the Bay of Cattaro and Sebenico. The results were all the more important as they were obtained despite the improvised nature of the agreements signed and the fact that the Germans were simultaneously attacking "non-cooperative" Italian units in the Adriatic including the destroyer *Sella* and gunboat *Aurora*, torpedoed by *S 54* and *61* in separate attacks, the corvette *Berenice* at Trieste, and the torpedo boats *Sirtori* and *Stocco* off Corfu. Under these circumstances and due to the fact that some vessels subsequently deserted the German cause, the "cooperating" units later had their status guaranteed by the on-board presence of armed German guards.

At the end of September during the German re-occupation of Dalmatia MAS boats covered a landing by German and Italian forces on the small island of Ugliano opposite Zara. This was an action of modest scope but noteworthy because it followed the failure of a German force carried on eight requisitioned Croatian fishing boats that tried to land in rubber dinghies under the automatic weapon fire of Partisans.

This cycle of operations continued during October. The consolidation of the position opposite Zara was, in addition to the MAS boats, the work of two large motorsail vessels, *Sant'Eufemia* and *San Simeone*, armed at the initiative of the now isolated city's local authorities with a 47-mm/32 antitank rifle and some machine guns. Joined later by a pair of small motorboats they fought engagements with armed Partisan boats on 2, 3, 5 and 27 October.

Meanwhile, the Italian vessels from Albania had moved into the upper Adriatic joining there the Italian gunboat *Lido*, tug *Grado*, the armed steamships *Nazario Sauro*, *Jadera*, *San Giorgio*, and *San Salomone*; the armed yacht *Cervo*, from the Ionian islands; the auxiliary minesweepers *Traù*, *Littorio*, *Adria*, *Balilla*, and *Vittorio Bruno*, the tug *Colonnello Pozzi* and other assorted auxiliaries from Venice; and six patrol boats of the Regia Guardia di Finanza. These vessels "cooperated" on the initiative of their commanders and always on the basis of the decision taken on 10 September 1943 by General Gastone Gambara, commander of the Italian army group in eastern Italy and future chief of staff of the fascist republic army, who had also decided to continue the war alongside the Germans.

11. *A 1944 poster that reads: "The German soldier fights for the freedom of our sea." It was intended to encourage Italian workers. (Enrico Cernuschi)*

On 21 September the equivocal nature of the cooperation agreements and the evolution of events caused *Pola* to flee to Brindisi followed, five days later by the torpedo boat *Pilo* and the tug *Porto Conte*, which headed south at night after neutralizing their German guards. They had been part of the escort of a convoy of five merchantmen that were being transferred from Durazzo to Trieste together with *Arborea*, which was loaded with troops of the Brennero Division, and an alpine brigade which later formed the nucleus of the Social Republic's Littorio and Monte Rosa divisions. These events, along with an engine failure experienced by the torpedo boat *Missori* on 6 October-- that the Germans attributed to sabotage--sharpened tension between the Germans and the "cooperating" Italian units in the Adriatic. However, Germany's continuing lack of men and ships and a new fiasco which occurred on 5 October off the Sabbioncello Peninsula when two armed partisan motorsailors broke up a German and Croat landing, forced the Germans to make the best of a bad situation. It was an inevitable choice as their Adriatic "fleet" had already been reduced in an attack on Valona roads on the night of 21 September by the British warships *MTB 85*, *89*, *287*, *290*, and *295* that sank the small auxiliary cruiser *Rovigno* at the cost of some damage to *MTB 295*, which hit an underwater obstruction during the action.[16]

Germany's last two operational S-boats transferred from the Adriatic to the Aegean in early October to support operations to reconquer the islands British troops had occupied. In the meanwhile the Axis presence in the middle and lower Adriatic was reduced to just the three Italian MAS and the torpedo boat *T 7* after a German coastal battery erroneous sank *Sant'Eufemia*, on 13 October, British aircraft strafed *Goffredo Mameli* on passage to the upper Adriatic on 27 October, and *San Simeone*'s engine breakdown at Gravosa on the 29th, and her bombing and subsequent loss. In that same period the British navy began to operate a flotilla of modern destroyers out of Brindisi and on 16 October a squadron of British MTBs moved to Lissa Island in the middle Adriatic.

A renewed German landing on the Sabbioncello Peninsula succeeded on 23 October contemporaneously with the occupation of the port of Ploce, helped by support of *T 7*'s guns. This, however, did not calm German suspicions against their erstwhile partners and from this period they showed a marked preference for Croatian over Italian support. In October, after restoring control over the waters of Quarnaro, first threatened by Chetniks, who believed a British landing was imminent, and a little later by Tito's forces, the composite Italian flotilla's last large enterprise occurred on 13 November when it landed German troops on Cherso, Lussino, and Veglia islands, which were reconquered in a matter of hours.

The disappearance of *MAS 431*, lost without a trace in November 1943 and the 19 November mutiny of *MAS 433*, which joined the Royal forces after the murder of her captain, definitely killed the accords of 10 September.[17] From early November the progressive entry into service under German

---

[16] Pope, *Flag 4*, 154-55.
[17] Ufficio Storico della Marina Militare, *Navi perdute*, Volume II, 140, states that MAS 431 was sunk during a "naval action between Zara and Sebenico." This action is not mentioned in any of the literature known to the authors.

colors of various ex-Italian units immobilized or under repair at the time of the Armistice and taken over in northern harbors, the transfer from France to Fiume of a company of Küstenjäger, troops specialized in special amphibious operations with their own mechanized column of motorboats, and the simultaneous deployment of two army engineers battalions equipped with dozens of smaller landing craft, finally enabled the Germans to finish on their own the occupation of the remaining enemy-controlled islands in the Dalmatian archipelago, an enterprise largely finished by the following March.

At the end of November the Kriesgmarine took over *MAS 430*, but she was damaged in an air attack on 6 December 1943 at Sebenico and paid off at the end of that year. The torpedo boat *T 7*, which was also in poor condition, was likewise paid off, but rearmed eight months later and entrusted to a Croatian crew. On 15 November the Germans "asked" the Marina Repubblicana and the Salò government for the cession of *MAS 522*, the gunboats *Gallipoli* and *Otranto*, the minelayers *Albona* and *Rovigno*, the auxiliary minesweepers *Piave* and *Chiesa*, and the minesweeper *RD 35*, whose crews had chosen, after the armistice, to continue the war in the Aegean with the old ally on the basis of an agreement similar to that in the Adriatic. Up to that point the Italian ships located in Greece which remained associated with Germany had conducted only coastal patrols because the Kriegsmarine did not face in Hellenic waters any emergencies as in the Adriatic and the Italian crews refused to fight against their compatriots in the Dodecanese

By year's end the organization of the Italian Republic Navy was finally settled. The small Italian vessels still active in the upper Adriatic were grouped into a unit called *Gruppo Dragaggio Venezia* (Venice Minesweeping Group) that shared the shield of the German *Hafenschutzflottille* based in that lagoon city. The Marina Repubblicana also controlled the many jointly-manned coastal batteries of that area, and the defensive perimeter of the town with some units detached at Trieste, Pola, and Zara.

The Decima MAS deployed the fast coastal forces in the Tyrrhenian Sea under general German control, which did not influence the planning and command of operations and training. As Borghese was directing an organization that would soon grow to 10,000 men he no longer commanded the MAS boats and special attack craft personally. The leadership of these units passed to Lieutenant Commander Mario Arillo, like Borghese, a holder

12. *Partisans captured by Italian black-shirts from Zara after the landing on Isola Grossa, 2 October 1943. (Editrice Militare Italiana)*

of the Medaglia d'oro (Italy's highest award). His exploits included the sinking of the British cruiser *Bonaventure* on 31 March 1941, and the forcing of Algiers harbor with his submarine *Ambra* where a group of gamma swimmers (frogmen) sank a freighter and damaged three others. The choice proved sound as Arillo effectively led his small force until the last day of the war. The Decima MAS had in the Adriatic another offensive branch which was formed by some MTBs and by the future Adriatic midget submarine flotilla.

In the meanwhile the Varignano's Antisom antisubmarine warfare school, which operated the submarine chasers, *Equa, Capodistria, La Santa Maria*, and *Antonio Landi* cooperated with the German coastal forces in the Tyrrhenian Sea under the direction of Marina Repubblicana staff--soon nicknamed *Marina nera* (Black Navy) due to the officers' habit of wearing the traditional dark blue uniform while Borghese and his men preferred the San Marco Marine regiment green. Many auxiliary ships recorded in Appendix II and scattered throughout Italy's northern harbors performed their usual duties under the Marina nera's direction. The ministry, based at Montecchio

Maggiore, near Vicenza, controlled the remaining land organization and the various inspectorates. The naval infantry, all under the orders of Borghese, increased constantly sending at first two battalions and an artillery battery to Anzio on 3 March 1944 (flanking there an Italian Air Force paratrooper brigade, two Italian SS battalions and some minor units) and growing later to a division-sized formation whose battalions were employed against Italian partisans in the summer of 1944, then against the French in the Alps, and later along the Italian eastern border facing Tito's partisans before being grouped against the British along the Gothic line in early 1945. Intelligence, including code breaking, and attack craft training were concentrated in Borghese's hands. See Appendix I for the organization of the Marina Repubblicana.

Chapter 5. Anzio and Nettuno

In the Tyrrhenian Sea the fledging Marina Repubblicana, specifically the Decima Flottiglia MAS, undertook its first offensive operations against Allied forces. Borghese bought to the Germans a dowry of the 28 ton MAS boats, *MAS 531*, *556*, and *562*, all under repair, and a dozen 3 ton MTSM (*motoscafo turismo silurante modificato*) type attack craft armed with a 450-mm torpedo. There were also some MTM (*motoscafo turismo modificato*) explosive boats and underwater teams with their SLC manned torpedoes and CA type midget submarines. The tiny submarines, however, were nearly useless because their transport boats, *Murena*, *Sparide*, and *Grongo* had been scuttled at Spezia on the afternoon of 9 September.

On 26 October the Decima MAS, received four more MAS boats and the three scuttled submarines, which needed to be raised, repaired, and refitted. This increase in strength was followed on 8 November 1943 by the assignment of two 60 ton MS (*motosiluranti*) type motor torpedo boats and another four MAS, enough to form three squadrons, along with the promise to transfer the motor fishing vessels *Pegaso* and *Cefalo* and nine landing craft (MZ *704*, *706*, *744*, *777*, *785*, *799*, *703*, *736*, and *759*) to be used for auxiliary tasks, a promise that was only partially kept.

German generosity, certainly greater than that shown in the previous month to the Marina Repubblicana's Admiral Legnani and his successor Commander Ferrini, was completely self-interested. By November 1943, the campaigns in Sicily and the southern Tyrrhenian Sea had convinced the Kriegsmarine that classic motor torpedo boat tactics were no longer practical in the Western Mediterranean, given the clear preponderance of the enemy's aviation and their swarms of radar-equipped patrol boats, minesweepers and other coastal craft. At this point, the German S-boats, which were more suitable to the conditions prevailing in the Adriatic, were being trucked from Genoa to the Po. The ex-Italian torpedo boats and destroyers armed by the Germans along Italy's western coast would be reserved mostly for mine laying and defensive patrols, rather than offensive operations except in a few special cases between December 1943 and March 1945. This left the burden of offensive surface operations along the Tyrrhenian coastline in the hands of the Decima Flottiglia MAS.

The German approach to operations in the Western Mediterranean reflected its *Kuestenvorfeld* or coastal warfare doctrine conceived prewar and adopted in Western Europe from 1941. It dictated a series of rings--the

13. *Admiral Giuseppe Sparzani, Marina Repubblicana chief of staff from February 1944, saluting the Battalion Barbarigo's teenage mascots before the unit's departure to Anzio. (Storia Militare)*

outermost blue water ring consisted of submarines and bombers tasked with attacking the enemy's traffic as far from the coast as possible. The outer ring of the coastal defensive layer consisted of fast motor torpedo boats to threaten the enemy's warships and, if possible, traffic. The next ring consisted of offensive (if possible) and defensive minefields. Then came an inner ring of escort ships, sub chasers, minesweepers, and gunboats which guarded

Germany's vital coastal traffic. Finally shore batteries and special troops with a limited amphibian capacity defended the coasts themselves.

The practice of Kuestenvorfeld in the Western Mediterranean after the Italian armistice roughly followed this pattern. German submarines were able to transit the Straits of Gibraltar until April 1944 and had, between September 1943 and August 1944, an average of nine boats present in the theater with at best a third serviceable. They achieved their last success in May 1944 and the last six were lost, by bombing or scuttling, at Toulon in August 1944. The

14. *A rounded bilge allowed the MTSM and SMA boats to maintain slightly higher speeds in rough weather than the 10-12 knots the hard-chine, double-stepped hulled MAS boats could make. (Sergio Nesi via Storia Militare)*

Luftwaffe, armed with its new guided missiles, was more effective, but in June 1944 the invasion of Normandy forced overnight a massive redeployment of air strength to northern France leaving the job of harassing Allied traffic, both in the Western and Eastern Mediterranean, until the war's end to a lone torpedo bomber group of the Italian fascist republic air force which began its operations in March 1944 at Anzio.

Regardless of the propaganda demands expressed on 14 November 1943 by Mussolini to Borghese: "You must very quickly get a success at sea, however small, so we may publish our first war bulletin." the naval plan agreed between Italian and German was elementary in its linearity: assume the offensive with the fast coastal forces, which were few and of smaller size

15. *SMA training at Spezia, spring 1944. (Sergio Nesi via Storia Militare)*

compared to the dozens of U.S. and British motor torpedo boats and gunboats present in the Tyrrhenian Sea, and contest the enemy traffic and force them to maintain or, better yet, increase the coastal assets in theater.[18] In this kind of naval guerrilla war the first duty was simply to endure and to engage the enemy forces as much as possible while waiting for something new, east or west, military or political, that would change the course of events.

---

[18] Bordonga, *Borghese e la X Flottiglia MAS*, 61.

16. *Launching a Neger at Anzio 20 April 1944 (*Drawing *by Franco Harrauer)*

Following an intense preparatory phase the first "inner ring" unit to deploy operationally in the Tyrrhenian Sea was an MTSM type torpedo motorboat squadron at Spezia on 25 December 1943. There followed over the next week three successful missions to insert agents into Sardinia to work with local republican parties and clandestine fascist organizations. Thereafter the real war for the Decima MAS (and the Marina Repubblicana) was the one against the Anglo-Americans, notwithstanding elements that deployed in the Black Sea, in shore batteries along the Atlantic coast, in chemical units in German harbors, and even in China.

A squadron of four MTSMs was trucked to Terracina in January 1944 to conduct night attacks in the Gulf of Naples against enemy merchant shipping. Borghese had deployed these 3 ton speedboats in the Mediterranean and Black seas since 1942 and one had even scored a success off the Egyptian coast against the British Hunt destroyer *Eridge* on 29 August 1942.

The MTSMs conducted four night forays between 17 and 21 January. There were no results and in the second mission *MTSM 302* was lost after a collision with *MTSM 226*. Allied forces, in fact, never noticed the sorties of these tiny motorboats even though the crews had the impression that fire was twice directed against them.

17. *The water column of a 50-kg anti-ship bomb dropped by a SMA during a training exercise, spring 1944. (Sergio Nesi via Storia Militare)*

It would have been better to send the MTSMs to attack an anchored target, for this was what the assault craft had been designed to do. In fact, such a plan was drawn up. The attack would have been launched from Terracina at the end of May by four torpedo motorboats of the SMA type (short for MTSMA or *Motoscafo da Turismo Silurante Modificato Allargato*, a slightly larger two-man MTB) and four MTM explosive boats. However, the Allied breaking of the Gustav Line forced the plan's cancellation.

The next action occurred off Anzio on the night of 22 January after the squadron was hastily moved from Terracina to Fiumicino following the unexpected Allied landings that morning. Three Italian MTSM boats sallied against the British and American protective squadron (a force of about sixty coastal minesweepers, motor launches, and submarine chasers). *MTSM 226*, piloted by Petty Officer First Class Amleto Tornissi, dropped a pair of anti-ship bombs--a modified depth charge that had a positive thrust which allowed

18. *Commander Borghese and Admiral Sparzani at Spezia, 26 February 1944. (Storia Militare)*

it to float for three to four seconds after launch, in the path of a pursuing vessel. He witnessed an explosion and claimed the sinking of an enemy corvette. The torpedoes fired at a destroyer by each of the boats, however, "failed." Once again the Allies did not notice this stealthy attack and attributed the commotion to a lone German bomber. On the return to base *MTSM 206*'s engine failed and her crew scuttled her with hand grenades. *MTSM 226*'s Tornissi experienced the same predicament "as a result of bad weather [the] craft was . . . thrown on the beach suffering irreparable damage."[19] *MTSM 304*'s second pilot, Petty Officer Pisu, was wounded in his right foot by shrapnel from the blind barrage the Anglo-Americans fired into the sky that night.

The loss of these Decima MAS units, no matter how unpleasant, was taken for granted by the flotilla's command and even considered acceptable given the vulnerability of the little boats and the ability of Italian industry to easily mass produce them delivering, by April 1945, to Germany and Italy, more than 120 small torpedo motorboats and at least 143 MTM explosive boats. In that same period, a levy of volunteers was enrolled in the new school of Sesto Calende which graduated about two hundred operators, about a third German. Thus, men and equipment were never a worry to the commanders of the Decima MAS. What mattered at that stage was for Italy to undertake at least some naval activity. In fact, Admiral Meendsen-Bohlken transmitted a telegram of congratulations that stated: "The first operational mission of your flotilla gives me the opportunity to express my admiration. The mission is a good omen for the further reconstruction and combative use of the reborn Italian navy advancing the prosperity of Italy and the achievement of final victory. Hail the Decima Flottiglia MAS!"[20] It cost Meendsen-Bohlken a lot to say this. He had been openly hostile to the Italian navy during his first term as naval liaison and, as recorded by the German consul in Rome, Eitel Friedrich Möllhausen: ". . . [He] did not want to be considered by Dönitz, too acquiescent toward the Italian navy like his predecessor, Admiral Ruge." Moreover, the admiral judged Borghese too proud and independent.[21]

While the Fiumicino squadron waited for more MTSMs and the next new moon at the end of February before again venturing into the waters off Anzio, an unexpected source enhanced the Decima MAS's effectiveness. Admiral Franco Maugeri, former head of the Regia Marina's intelligence service, had infiltrated a pair of agents who joined the Decima MAS as technicians. In an attempt to underline his importance in the various spying initiatives, often quite amateur, that had sprung up like mushrooms in Rome

---

[19] Nesi, *Decima*, 158.
[20] Bordogna, *Borghese e la X Flottiglia MAS*, 76.
[21] Möllhausen, *La carta perdente*, 402.

after that city's occupation, Maugeri pushed their reports and began to extol the efficiency and the threat posed by Borghese's men.

19. *PC-626 and SMA 318 clash off Anzio. (Drawing by Franco Harrauer)*

On the night of 20/21 February three MTSMs finally sortied. The motto, scratched by a sailor on the side of one of the truck transports that brought the boats from Spezia roughly translated as: "small bow big arrow." This captured the strategic reality of their war: it was the only form of surface attack the Axis could deploy on the Tyrrhenian Sea against such a vastly superior foe.

On the 20th a few minutes before midnight *MTSM 216*, piloted by Sergeant Rocco Chiarello and Seaman Candiollo Guido, launched against "a big destroyer" and observed an explosion. Some sources have identified this as the Royal Navy's *LST 305* of 2,366 tons, which was torpedoed and sunk that day, but the event's timing indicates that credit must be given to *U 230*. As *MTSM 216* withdrew she crossed an enemy unit that she identified as a gunboat and flung two 40-pound anti-ship bombs into the vessel's path.

These provoked a lively Allied reaction that occurred as the boat withdrew. *MTSM 216* returned to port unharmed but *MTSM 304* was damaged during the sortie. *PC 621* reported engaging five targets that night, destroying an MS type torpedo boat ("upon observing shell hits on target, target exploded and was observed leaving huge water spout and smoke mass.") and chasing another up the coast for an hour.[22]

A mission by three MTSMs in those same waters on the night of 22 February was, conversely, the victim of an immediate and precise U.S. reaction enabled by a radar sighting of the Italian craft by *PC 627* from 2,400 yards. She closed and discovered three boats. She engaged one that passed just 200 hundred yards down the starboard side; another was off the port bow

20. *Awards for X MAS and German veterans from Anzio, 20 July 1944. (Storia Militare)*

and the third headed straight toward the patrol boat and "swung sharp to the right and passed within a few yards of our port quarter, getting out of sight before fire was opened." *PC 627* swung hard to starboard but lost sight off all the enemy craft. However, her radar allowed her to continue to track the elusive enemy and a half hour later at 2150 another boat passed to starboard. "Fire was opened with three 20 MMs, 3"/50 and 40 MM at very close range." The target, which was *MTSM 236*, disintegrated. The two operators, Ensign Bruno Solari and Seaman Renato Paris, were the first Decima MAS members of the Republican Navy lost at sea. *PC 627*'s fire forced *MTSM 208* to beach

---

[22] *PC 621*, "Report of Action 20/21 February."

herself. Subsequently damaged by a German coastal battery, wave action destroyed *MTSM 208* the next day. The 280-ton American sub chaser expended 510 20-mm, 46 40-mm, and 15 3-inch rounds during the action.[23]

On the night of 24 February five MTSM and SMAs sortied. They did not find any targets and during their return a German observation post near Castel Porziano fired on them and wounded one operator.

On the evening of 1 March three newly arrived Italian MAS boats made a foray from Civitavecchia but sighted nothing. Negative results occurred in subsequent sorties on the nights of 3, 5 (when a German battery damaged *MAS 502*), and 6 March (when a German MFP fired in error on *MAS 531* and *561* causing minor damage and wounding an Italian sailor). The Italian sailors kept striking deserted seas because mounting Allied air superiority made daytime navigation a better choice for the average daily run of six LSTs and assorted LCTs supplying the Anzio beachhead. They considered the threat of coastal artillery fire less dangerous than the possibility of nocturnal torpedo ambushes.

After two more missions by MAS boats on the 9th and 14th of March struck empty waters the MTBs adopted a new tactic. On their next sortie they deployed alongside the small torpedo boats. The idea was to use the noisy engines of the MAS boats to lure away the enemy's defensive screen leaving the way open for the smaller and stealthier SMA to attack the LSTs and Liberty ships clustered inshore. The Decima MAS attempted the first action of this kind on the night of 18 March. *PC 545* on "anti E-Boat" patrol picked up *SMA 316* from 900 yards at 2320 on 18 March. She opened fire at 2324 after two challenges went unanswered. The small torpedo boat started to zigzag at high speed and a ten minute chase followed until a round hit the gasoline tank and triggered an explosion that raised a column of water "approximately fifty feet." Ensign Gianfranco Pizzigalli and Petty Officer Cortese Ricci died in the action. *MAS 531* also came under fire and received minor damage. *PC 545* expended 330 20-mm and 10 40-mm rounds. The Americans recovered Pizzigalli's body and thus learned that their foe had been The Decima Flottiglia MAS.[24]

---

[23] *PC-627*, "Action Report against E-Boats, 22 February 1944."
[24] *PC-545*, "Action Report, 18 March 1944."

On the evening of 25 March MAS and SMA boats again sortied in tandem. *MAS 504* attacked after sighting an enemy formation only to be surrounded by a section of U.S. PT boats recently sent from Corsica to Anzio as a more nimble deterrent against the fast Italian craft. The small torpedo boat hit *PT 207* with her fire but was, in turn, immobilized and then rammed and sunk by the British destroyer *Grenville*.

Despite these negative results the MAS boats made renewed efforts on 3, 5, and 13 April without sighting any targets. On the night of 20 April three SMA came in contact with the Allied screen and two boats launched torpedoes. Despite the violent enemy reaction the Italian boats escaped unharmed and *SMA 312* piloted by Ensign Fulk Baglioni claimed a hit on a corvette. That same night off Anzio the Germans attempted their first surface coastal offensive action of the year in the Western Mediterranean launching two dozen brand new Neger semi-submersible attack craft. Ten were lost for no return. They did not repeat the Neger experiment in the Mediterranean.

The night of 30 April was the turn of *MAS 557* and *561*, which clashed with two groups of PT boats. In a close-range exchange of fire three PTs suffered "superficial damage" while hitting both Italian torpedo boats. *MAS 557* was immobilized and finally beached at Ostia, where she was destroyed the next day.[25] Further unsuccessful MAS sorties followed on 5, 7, and 9 May.

On the night of 13 May German coastal radar sighted some targets prompting a mission by three SMA despite the full moon. They ran into *PC 627* and *PC 1226*. *PC 627*, about a thousand yards astern detected the intruders from 900 yards at 0057 on 14 May. She wasted little time opening fire with three 20-mm, a 40-mm and a 30 cal. machine gun. After seven minutes she "ceased firing, closed target which was found crippled and dead in the water. . . . One of the crews' body was hanging over the gunwale, another floating in the water, both lifeless." This was *SMA 308*. Petty Officer Giovanni Guareschi died but Ensign Valdo Pietra was only wounded and was subsequently rescued. The American ship expended 485 rounds of 20-mm, 14 40-mm, and two 3-inch shells.[26]

---

[25] Nesi, *Decima*, 174.
[26] *PC-627*, "Action Report, 14 May 1944."

21. *Borghese at Anzio, March 1944. (Storia Militare)*

SMA 314 and *318* piloted by Lieutenant Sergio Nesi and petty officer Cesare Zironi ran afoul of *PC 626*. Her radar detected the SMAs at 0157 and the American ship closed to 700 yards before making visual contact. The SMAs then separated. Nesi, under fire from the submarine chaser, cut sharply to port across *PC 626*'s bow and dropped an anti-ship bomb. According to the ship's report, "A large explosion occurred dead ahead. It shook the ship a bit, and threw up a sheet of water that cleared the radar dome atop the main mast." Firing with all guns, *PC 626* chased *SMA 318* which was trailing smoke. She emerged into the clear after ten minutes to find the target lost to sight and radar. On this basis *PC 626* concluded she had sunk the small torpedo boat. In fact Nesi returned unscathed to base along with *SMA 314*.[27]

An unproductive patrol by motor torpedo boats on 21 May was followed by another sortie on the night of the 23th by *SMA 306* and *318*. American radar picked up the two boats at 0010 on the 24th from 3,000 yards. *PC 626* turned to close and made visual contact at 0016. She challenged twice and

---

[27] Nesi, "Chiaro di luna," 37-38. *PC-626*, "Action Report, 14 May, 1944."

then fired star shell. This caused the Italian boats to take evasive maneuvers and the American warship opened fire with all guns. The range was a thousand yards. "For the next 10 minutes it was a game of hide and seek, with the target darting in and out of the heavy smoke, and with us firing on it whenever a star shell lit it up." At 0052 *SMA 318* dashed into view and tried to lay an anti-ship bomb in the PC's path. The American turned hard to starboard to avoid this threat and the SMA slid down the ship's port side, struck the propeller guard and released a bomb. The intense point-blank fire that followed disabled *SMA 318*. *PC 626* closed and found "the boat dead in the water with no one aboard." She put a raft into the water to rescue Ensign Francesco Loda and Seaman Luigi Taiti. The American ship expended 750 20-mm, 48 40-mm, and 28 3-inch rounds. *SMA 306* returned to port.[28]

On 29 May there was a brief encounter between a U.S. Navy PT boat and *MAS 562*. The Italian unit outran her opponent and escaped undamaged.

The Decima MAS finally departed the waters off Anzio after the occupation of Rome on 4 June. As a result of its first campaign it suffered the loss of sixteen MTSM and SMA boats, the majority to accidents. Nonetheless, this seemed positive compared to the results believed obtained and in the context of the type of naval warfare being fought by the Axis along the coast of Naples and Lazio.

---

[28] *PC-626*, "Action Report, 24 May 1944."

Chapter 6. Elba and Provence

With the cracking of the Gustav line and the Allied drive into central Italy the maritime theater of operations shifted north. On the night of 30 May *MAS 531* and *562* ferried to the island of Giglio a German raiding party that attacked a U.S. Army detachment stationed there. Between the 17th and 20th of the month a French division conquered the island of Elba from a small German and Italian garrison. Finally, overcoming the losses of material suffered when the Decima MAS abandoned its base at Fiumicino, the MAS boats resumed offensive operations in Tuscan waters with an unsuccessful patrol on the night of 23 June

On the night of 29 June *MAS 531* and *562* tried to penetrate Portoferraio to torpedo a merchant ship anchored there. However, *PT 308* and *309* on a routine patrol out of Bastia detected the units and intervened. The MAS boats fled to the north and in the course of a running fight an American 40-mm

22. *Borghese and Lieutenant Commander Mario Arillo who assumed operational command of the attack units from Borghese. (Mursia)*

shell struck *MAS 562*'s fuel tank and ignited a fire. Fearing an explosion the fourteen crew members abandoned ship and were picked up by the Americans. The next morning *PT 306* returned to the scene and discovered *MAS 562* still afloat. Apparently the automatic security system had extinguished the fire and thus *PT 306* was able to tow the boat to Bastia. The Americans turned the MAS over to the Regia Marina on 12 July 1944.

MAS boats waited in ambush off Meloria on the night of 7 July but saw nothing sightings. The next new moon witnessed a novelty when on the night of 31 July two German SMAs deployed for the first time, in the company of

23. *The auxiliary sub chaser CS13 Antonio Landi at Spezia.* (Storia Militare)

an Italian SMA. This signaled a Kriegsmarine decision to adopt Italian doctrine and boats adding them to the novel attack craft they had been hastily developing since 1943. The action, repeated the next night by the same three units, had no operational consequences, but it marked the beginning of mixed-nationality sorties by surface assault craft which became more common, although still not the rule as demonstrated by an unproductive sortie conducted entirely by the Decima MAS on the night of August 9.

24. *The establishment of the Servizio Ausiliario Femminile (Female Auxiliary Service) was one of the novelties of the fascist Republic. The Decima MAS branch had about female 1,000 volunteers. (Uniformi e Armi)*

The Allied landings in Provence on 15 August 1944 were unstoppable from the beginning. To contest them at sea the German navy only had one operational submarine and some corvettes and auxiliary escorts based at Toulon and Marseilles and in the offensive's first days U.S. destroyers sank four of these warships. Trying to emulate the actions of the Decima MAS off Anzio the Kriegsmarine deployed four ex-Italian MAS boats, which had entered German service in July 1944, and two additional MAS boats recovered at Toulon and previously employed ferrying agents to Corsica for German intelligence. Five of these units, *SA 12, 13, 17, 18*, and *19*, previously *MAS 549, 551, 558, 424* (II), and *437*, were sent literally into the meat grinder on the night of 17 August, encountering the American destroyers *Satterlee*,

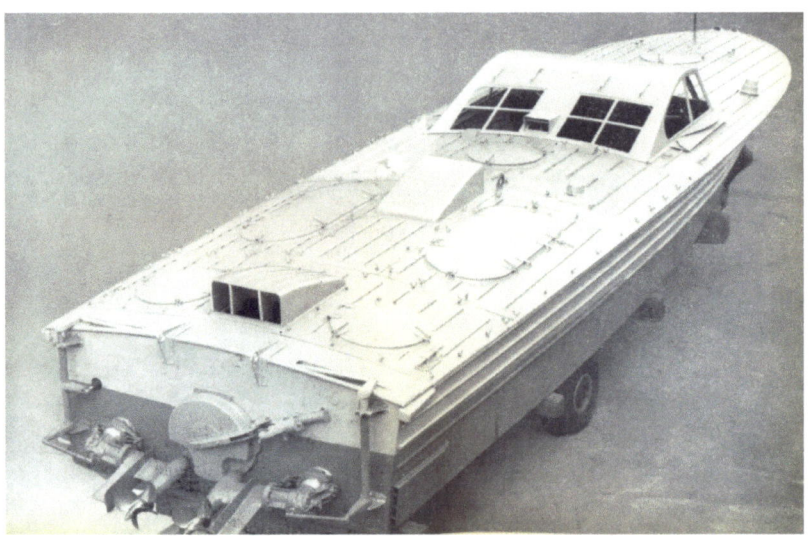

25. *An SMA attack craft built for the Germans by Cattaneo Cabi of Milan. It was nearly identical to the Italian models. (Storia Militare)*

Harding, Frankford, and *Carmick* off Saint Tropez. Warned by radar the American warships sank all five of the German attackers.

The Kriegsmarine next sent four ex-Italian VAS boats (60 ton, twenty knot antisubmarine vessels) one of which, *RA 252*, was manned by Marina Repubblicana personal, as motor torpedo boats in the Gulf of Juan, between Antibes and Cannes. On the night of 21 August four USN destroyers sank the German *RA 251, 255,* and *259* in two separate actions. *Hughes* first picked up the German force at 0110 from 9,000 yards. She closed at high speed, illuminated, at opened fire at 0123 from 2,300 yards. One boat was quickly overwhelmed by a deluge of 5-inch and 40-mm fire and two of the German crew rescued. The others took fled to shallow water in the Gulf of Juan where the destroyers *Champlin* and *Nields* joined *Hughes* and *Hilary P. Jones* in hunting them down. After dawn *Jones* saw one of the boats on the beach and shelled it until her "fire caused the boat to catch fire and blow up with a tremendous blast."[29] *Hughes,* which inflicted most of the damage expended 364 5-inch

---

[29] Charles F. Hughes, "Action Report, 21 August, 1944". *Hilary P. Jones,* "Action Report, 21 August 1944."

rounds, 380 40-mm, and 526 20-mm. This outcome killed any idea of using the former Italian fast coastal units still available, leaving the scene open only to the Italian and German special attack craft and the Decima MAS's last surviving MAS squadron.

On the morning of 24 August two Italian SMA boats, operating for the first time with three Decima MAS MTM explosive motorboats, left their new base at Villafranca to search for the enemy. In addition, four German SMAs sortied that evening. The considered decision to use the MTM as an attack craft, even though the type had been designed to attack vessels at anchor or in port, and that only with great luck and perfect conditions did it have a chance of hitting a moving target, confirmed the deteriorating Axis situation. During that night the two Italian and one German SMA unsuccessfully attacked what they thought were four American destroyers off Cap Ferrat. The motorboats all returned to base undamaged. The next night the three PT flotillas in the area received orders to erect an impenetrable barrier against the Axis assault craft, incorrectly referred to as "Linsen" types like those previously encountered in Northern France.

On 25 August Axis two formations ventured out. The first consisted of four Italian SMA boats and the second the Italian *SMA 3*, a German SMA boat, and four Italian MTMs. PTs sighted the first group off Cap Ferrat and the four SMAs dropped smoke floats and retreated under the cover of the resulting fog. In the second group a mechanical failure forced the German MTB to abort but *SMA 3*, manned by Ensign Carlo Sicola and Seaman Giuliano Gregorat, continued and encountered off Villafranca the large French destroyer *Le Fantasque* bombarding the coastal radar stations of Cap Ferrat and Mont Boron. The tiny craft attacked, reported an explosion, and claimed a success. At dawn the next day observers reported a big destroyer stopped offshore, which seemed to confirm *SMA 3*'s claims and provided welcome material for the fascist propaganda mill. However, the French destroyer was undamaged. In fact, her record for that night does not even mention the attack.[30]

Two Italian SMAs and four MTMs along with a similar German formation ventured out on the night of 26 August. The Italians did not

---

[30] Carré, *Le Fantasque*, 329-30. The ship stopped twice, at 2030 and 2114, "waiting for a boat that followed with the mail."

register any contacts while the Germans recorded an action with American PT boats without damage to either side. That same night *PT 210* and *213* reported that they engaged a column of five explosive boats and that four blew up after they opened fire.

Another mixed Italo-German sortie occurred on the night of 28 August. One of the German SMAs tangled with a PT boat. The German motorboat defended herself with a Panzerfaust and submachine guns and, although damaged, she returned to base. A similar outcome occurred two nights later with the loss of a German MTM and with the capture of the pilot by PT boats. On 30 August, American troops occupied Nice advancing the front to the old Franco-Italian border. This forced the small naval units to redeploy and brought Italian units under the fire of overactive German shore batteries that damaged an MTM. Another friendly fire incident occurred the next day during the transfer of units from Mentone to San Remo. The last action of the Provence campaign occurred on 5 September when the Germans deployed five semi submersibles of the new Marder type (launching difficulties prevented another seven from making it to sea). These 10.5 ton attack craft were more sophisticated than the Neger, but the results they obtained were no better and the destroyers USS *Ludlow* and the French *Le Malin* sank four of the five with depth charges and machine guns.

26. *Three photos of the Marina Repubblicana's submarine chaser VAS 263 taken at Spezia in the winter of 1944/45. (courtesy of Fabio Cordini)*

Chapter 7. The Ligurian Sea

In late September, after the Allied army was safely ashore and Marseilles captured, Vice Admiral H. Kent Hewitt, commander of the U.S. 8th Fleet, wrote: "The Mediterranean Campaign, as far as the Navy was concerned, seemed about over."[31] However, events proved his optimism to be greatly premature. The Axis retained the northern Italian coast including the major ports of Genoa and Spezia and, if anything, the naval guerrilla war in the Western Mediterranean intensified.

The Ligurian campaign's symbolic commencement, at least from the perspective of the Marina Repubblicana, occurred several weeks before Admiral Hewett's pronouncement when, on the night of 7 September, *MAS 531* and *561*, which had just arrived in Lerici, undertook their first patrol along the western Rivera. It was a small event in the annals of the war at sea but significant considering the date and the fact that a year after the armistice Italian sailors were still pushing through southern French waters fighting alongside the Germans. This small beginning heralded the start of a campaign that forced the Allies, against their wishes and expectations, to maintain a powerful fleet in the Ligurian Sea called Flank Force to guard Allied ports and shipping and to assert control over the Axis-held coastline and waters. At one point Flank Force included a battleship, five cruisers, more than a dozen destroyers, and dozens of minesweepers, patrol craft, and motor torpedo boats. Against them a few German torpedo boats plied the Tyrrhenian Sea laying defensive mine barriers and patrolling the Ligurian coast along with smaller Kriegsmarine and Italian escorts. It was the sorties of the Decima MAS and German small attack craft, however, that absorbed most of the attention of the Allied naval forces.

On the same night of 7 September three Italian SMA boats sortied in addition to two MAS. They encountered *PT 215* and *216* and in the resulting engagement the PTs damaged one of the Decima MAS boats. The American account speaks of two separate engagements and the destruction of five enemy explosive boats. The fact each side had such different perspectives of events was not remarkable given that these night encounters occurred at high speeds from platforms with low visibility. The American account further

---

[31] Cherpak, *Memoirs of Admiral Hewitt*, 203.

notes that "the second engagement was confused by a smokescreen laid by the enemy."[32]

The night of 9 September saw another Marder affair that followed the usual screenplay: fourteen German boats deployed and ten were easily sunk

---

[32] Bulkley, *At Close Quarters*, 336.

27. *An MTM explosive boat at the Sesto Calende training school in 1944. (Erminio Bagnasco collection)*

by the U.S. destroyers *Madison* and *Hilary P. Jones* assisted by PTs. The Americans suffered no damage.

On the night of 10 September it was the turn of the Germans to run afoul of the PT patrol. In the course of a mission conducted with Italian craft *PT 206* and *214* dispatched a German SMA. There was nothing to record during the Italian sorties of 12, 13, and 14 September made by small units, nor for a pair of missions by MAS boats on the 16th and 22nd.

On the night of 26 September the Kriegsmarine employed a new novelty craft: the Molch, a true midget electric submarine. Nine sailed and two came back. The destroyers USS *Madison* and the French *Forbin* dispatched the others. Although four Molch remained at Spezia until the end of the war (the Italian navy later recovered one for testing) these boats made no further attacks in the Mediterranean.

In October, despite worsening weather, the frequency of Italian and German special attack craft missions did not diminish. On the 2nd, 3rd, and 10th, Axis SMA and MTM boats sortied, engaging during the first of these missions the American destroyers *Benson* and *Gleaves*. *Gleaves* fended off several determined attacks off Imperia, even dropping depth charges against pursuing craft she identified as German crash boats. Her captain reported the destruction of three boats—a claim at least partially substantiated by the capture of two German operators and one MTM.

A sortie on the 20th produced no results. A mixed mission on the night of 23 October that included twenty German and six Italian MTMs had no success. The USS *Woolsey* encountered two MTMs after dawn, one abandoned and one half-afloat. She finished off one and the French destroyer *Le Fortuné* dispatched the other. The Allies rescued two operators. Neither destroyers nor the four U.S. minesweepers in the area that night recorded any surface actions. Nonetheless, the Germans lost four boats. The month closed with an unsuccessful mission on the 24th.

28. *MAS 561, at Imperia March 1945. (Storia Militare)*

On the night of 7 November Axis forces experimented with a new force mix to supplement those already tried: an MTM escort for German Marders. The semi-submersibles, which were piloted by volunteer operators, had not demonstrated an ability to navigate without losing their orientation and the MTMs were supposed to help them locate targets. However, this assistance did not lead to a successful operation for these microscopic vessels. The Marder experiment was repeated on the night of 18 November. Fifteen boats sailed and seven disappeared with no results. On that same night the Italians lost five MTM due to fog.

29. The Italian prototype of the K 3 semi-submarine motor boat tested at Spezia by the Germans in the autumn of 1944. (Drawing by Franco Harrauer)

Four nights later the Decima MAS finally returned to its original mission with an attempt to insert manned torpedoes of the SSB or *Siluro San Bartolomeo* type into the port of Leghorn, which had become the principal Anglo-American hub in the eastern Tyrrhenian. These were an improved descendent of the SLC, the weapon that sank two British battleships in 1941. On this occasion *SSB 3*, piloted by Lieutenant Augusto Jacobacci and Sergeant Toma and *SSB 4*, with Lieutenant Sergio Pucciarini and Petty Officer Bonato, were ferried to their destination by *MTL* (*Motoscafo da Turismo Lento*) *476* and *MCN 567*, with *SMA 501* operated by Lieutenant Commander Arillo himself. However, weather forced the mission's cancelation. A new effort against Livorno to be conducted this time by *gamma* swimmers carried to their destination by *SMA 501*, a slightly modified motor boat whose crew had long specialized in infiltration missions and the recovery of inserted agents, was also scrapped on 14 December again due to weather. Another effort against Livorno planned for March 1945 was cancelled for the same cause along with a project against Toulon.

While attempts to force enemy ports repeatedly proved vain, the sorties of the small motor torpedo boats continued. A mission conducted on 25 November failed to sight the enemy. Patrols made on 28 and 29 November by *MAS 531*, *556*, and *561* likewise proved fruitless. On 11 December a formation of French sub chasers intercepted these same boats south of Cannes. The Marine Nationale units were ex U.S Navy patrol boats and sub chasers used throughout 1943-44 in the Mediterranean at Tunisia, Salerno, Anzio, and the Rivera. The Americans finally ceded them to the French leaving the Marine Nationale with the thankless and dangerous drudgery of patrolling night after night in search of the enemy's mosquito fleet. *Sabre* (ex *PC 1248*) picked up the Italian intrusion on radar at 0105 and opened fire sixteen minutes later. In the course of the following melee a French shell hit *MAS 531*'s rudder. At 0237 the destroyers *Le Fortuné*, USS *Ludlow*, and the patrol boat *Cimeterre* fired on the other pair of MAS boats, but without results. At 0320 *Sabre* again came upon *MAS 531*, which was completely disabled, and rescued a Decima MAS officer, a German radio operator, and six wounded men. There were five bodies aboard. The sub chaser's attempt to tow the boat back to port failed when the MAS foundered and sank. The next morning off Mentone *Javelot* (ex *PC 1562*) rescued the pilot of a scuttled Italian MTM.[33]

A sortie of MAS and special attack craft made on the night of 16 December proved futile. The stubborn Germans launched fifteen Marder on the night of 18 December. Allied patrol forces destroyed eight and one beached at Mentone and was recovered by U.S. Army troops. On 31 December 1944, in the last use of these vessels, five Marder sailed, four returned and one was destroyed.

With the beginning of the new year the Italian and German torpedo and explosive speedboats began to more frequently transport informers and saboteurs to the French coast. Up to the end of the war Italian boats safely inserted twenty-eight men and women on these missions. On 4 January 1945, the Germans lost an SMA during a normal reconnaissance mission while on the following night an Italian MAS scouted for German torpedo boats on one of their coastal minelaying excursions. These activities were interspaced with

---

[33] Darrieus and Quéguiner, *Historique de la Marine française*, 278.

ordinary reconnaissance patrols as on the night of 6 January by *MAS 553* and *561* and sorties on the 15th, 17th, and 19th of the month.

On 9 January *Le Fortuné* engaged five German SMAs sinking two. On 10 January, on the other hand, that same destroyer conducted an intense night fire action that led to her being awarded a citation even though she shot into the shadows since no Italian or German, surface or underwater craft were, in fact, at sea. On the morning of 18 January *CH 105* (ex-USS *SC 676*) and *Cimeterre* (formerly *PC 1250*) engaged two SMAs (one Italian, one German) and two German MTMs and sank the German SMA and one of the MTMs. The frustration caused by this stubborn foe who against all reason persisted to dispute the use of the sea against an ultra-powerful opponent was suggested by one of the French captains who referred to the small boats as "enemy vermin."[34]

The use of Decima MAS's small units continued in early February, despite the growing gasoline crisis, a nearly full moon, and rough seas. No contacts developed during missions conducted on the 1st, 2nd, and 3rd of the month. On the night of 4 February, however, a German MTM reported an unsuccessful attack on an American destroyer. Subsequent missions of MAS and Italian and German assault craft on 5, 7, 8, and 12, February struck empty seas but on the 17th a Decima SMA and a PT boat briefly clashed.

During March there were fruitless sorties on the nights of the 7th and 11th as well as failed attempts by *MAS 561* and *553* to tow two German SMA boats on a mission to force the small port of Mentone.

During a night action on 15 March with *MAS 505* (given by the Germans to the Decima MAS three months before) and *MAS 566* the Italian sailors unknowingly stumbled onto an old acquaintance from the spring nights off Anzio, *PC 626* albeit this time under the French flag and with the new name of *Lansquenet*. The ship's change in flag, however, did not bring luck to the patrol boat's crew because the 20-mm fire of the two Italian MTBs caused some damage and wounded ten men including the captain, Corvette Captain Rouan, "gravely struck in the head" while the Italian units escaped without a scratch after the brief exchange of fire.[35]

---

[34] Dossier TT D 196, "*Montcalm*, 1 February 1945."
[35] Ibid., Prot. 99 EMI ORG du 17/3/45.

The little war on the Ligurian Sea did not diminish in intensity even in April. The sorties of MAS boats and surface assault craft continued as before, even if the alleged sinking of a boat by *CH 125* (formerly *SC 1043*) on the night on April 15th is not confirmed by Italian or German sources. What is documented is the serious damage to the French destroyer *Trombe* inflicted by Petty Officer Sergio Denti's *MTM 548* on the night of April 17. Denti's small boat was one of six MTMs and a single SMA that had sortied from San Remo. He managed to approach *Trombe* undetected and rammed his target causing "a violent explosion on the starboard side . . . that suddenly shook the vessel."[36] The French destroyer suffered twenty dead or missing and returned slowly to Toulon under the escort of the British destroyer *Meteor*. The damage was so great it was considered not worth repairing, and *Trombe* was sold for scrapping in December 1946.

The sheer number of Axis vessels still left and the fact they were sailing up to the campaign's end signified Flank Force's failure to deny to their German and Italian foes the use of coastal waters. This was brought home on 21 April 1945 by a comment in a report of the USS *Mackenzie* regarding excessive risk to larger units. ". . . This command believes that the destroyer patrol . . . should be discontinued; and the denying of the gulf of Genoa to the enemy should be left to air craft (sic) and PT-boats."[37] On 26 April United States Naval Forces Northwest African Waters endorsed this recommendation, but by that time the fighting was over.

Allied armies cracked the Axis defenses in Northern Italy on 20 April. Given the anticipated capture of their ports, the MAS and the assault craft in the German and Italian bases on the Tyrrhenian coast executed a long-planned final gesture even as the last serviceable destroyer and the four corvettes still manned by the Germans scuttled themselves in Genoa on the 24th together with the remaining minor vessels and auxiliaries.

The Kriegsmarine concentrated its remaining surface attack craft for a mass strike against Livorno, almost suicidal considering the strength of the harbor's gun emplacements, for the night of 23/24 April. Fifteen of seventeen MTMs and SMAs deployed were lost. The attack had no results.

---

[36] Saibene, *Les torpilleurs de 1500 tonnes*, 135.
[37] *Mackenzie*, "Action Report, 21 April 1944."

On that same night the Decima MAS brought out *MAS 553, 556*, and *561*. For their last mission the craft were ordered to search for targets offshore while the small MTM and SMAs were to force the ports of Ajaccio, Nice, Antibes, and Saint Tropez while one attack craft of each type demonstrated off San Remo in an attempt to distract the Allied patrol vessels. *MAS 553* and *556* experienced a quiet patrol, but *MAS 561* became separated from her mates due to a temporary defect. *PT 305* and *307* encountered her

30. *The French destroyer* Trombe *at Toulon summer 1945. The damage inflicted by the Decima MAS, visible in the hull below the forward mount, was never repaired. (Storia Militare)*

and a running fight ensued as the MAS boat turned to escape. At first her greater speed and an anti-ship bomb she dropped in her wake allowed the MAS to pull away, but just on the edge of 40-mm range a shell hit and immobilized the boat. The Americans, as reported by the section commander, Lieutenant (JG). Walter E. Powell, USNR, intended to board the MAS but the small unit's fire persuaded them to keep away and they blasted her with their 40-mms until the MTB exploded and sank with all hands.[38]

The Decima MAS's harbor forcing missions, conducted by fifteen boats, two of them German, had no results since the various ports were empty except for some fishing boats the Italians did not consider military targets. During their night approach two separate clashes with French patrol craft occurred during which *Lansquenet* and *CH 112* and *122* (formerly *SC 534*) destroyed two Italian MTMs and a German SMA near Cap d'Antibes.

On 24 April, after one last mission, conducted in broad daylight by *MAS 553* and *505* in a vain attempt to trace the crew of *MAS 561*, these two MAS, together with the *MAS 556*, were scuttled at Porto Maurizio. The war at sea in the Western Mediterranean was over.

31. PC 606 *turned over to the French as* Lansquent *had several brushes with the Decima MAS. She displaced 280 tons and was armed with one 3-inch/50 dual purpose gun, one 40-mm and three 20-mm and, had a speed of 20 knots. (Navsource)*

---

[38] Bulkley, *At Close Quarters*, 346.

Chapter 8. The Adriatic

On 13 January, 1944, the Germans permitted the Republican Navy to establish in the Adriatic the 1st *Motosiluranti* Section formed by *MS 41* and *75*. There was to have been a second section, but a U.S. bombing raid on Genoa on 16 January 1944 wrecked *MS 16* and *34*, the boats allocated to this unit.

On 12 February *MS 41* deployed from Ancona and began a series of mining missions along the coast of the Abruzzo, Marche, and Romagna regions of the Italian peninsula. Units participating in this activity would eventually include *MS 75* and two motor launches of the former Regia Guardia di Finanza. Though the end of 1944 these boats conducted just over a hundred missions in which they laid four mines at a time, all of German types. The only certain result was the mining of the British destroyer *Loyal* off the Pesaro breakwater on 12 October, 1944. This large and modern warship had her starboard engine displaced and 160 feet of platting blown in and was so severely damaged she was considered beyond repair. Other mining losses included the Greek LST *Lesvos* (ex-*LST 33*), *MGB 657*, the motor launch *ML 258*, and *BYMS 2053*. *BYMS 2011* was damaged, and the trawler *Coriolanus* and *ML 558* were sunk after the end of hostilities. However, these vessels suffered their damage between the mouths of the Po River and San Benedetto del Tronto and the mines may have been laid by the Italian units or placed by Kriegsmarine torpedo boats, or even from minefields dating from before the armistice.

The activities of the two Decima MAS *motosiluranti* in the Adriatic were modest, but should be compared to the number of German craft coastal present in that basin. The Kriegsmarine, in fact, given the exceptionally low level of the Po during the winter of 1943-1944, which for a few months blockaded at Piacenza the units being transferred from the Tyrrhenian Sea, was not capable of putting to sea more than three S-boats before April 1944. This force grew to four boats during that month and to five in May. Only from June onwards was it finally possible to deploy a dozen units, including new boats commissioned at Monfalcone and units available after the long and difficult transfer down the Po. In any case, these MTBs operated defensively behind the Dalmatian island chain.

32. *The Decima MAS MTB MS 75 with a German Linsen attack boat, September 1944. (Storia Militare)*

In March 1944 small submarines of the Italian CB type began operating from Pola. Their missions consisted mainly of landing informants beginning with an initial sortie successfully carried out off Termoli just after 14 March 1944. U.S. bombing raids, however, undermined the strength of the squadron so that, in practice, only one boat was constantly operational between May and September 1944. After September new units began to enter service permitting the deployment of a squadron with an average strength of four boats.

During the winter of 1943-1944 Decima MAS also attempted, on the initiative of Captain Angelo Belloni, the "father" of the diver concept, to modify the small assault boats *CA 1*, *3* and *4* present at Spezia adding two cages for external 450-mm torpedoes. In the end, however, only one unit, *CA 3*, was used between May and August 1944 by the Antisom escort flotilla for training German and Italian units in anti-submarine tactics.

The practice of inserting commandos behind enemy lines increased between July and October 1944 with seven missions performed by patrol and motorboats, in particular, *ML 32* and *34*, which successfully landed on five occasions commando teams belonging to the Decima "Ceccacci Group," a company of the NP (*Nuotatori e Paracadutisti*) battalion, which operated in uniform to avoid being treated as spies if captured. The majority of the raiders managed to return through the front line after performing their tasks.

After the occupation of Ancona, taken by Polish troops on 18 July 1944, German and Italian naval operations focused on attacks against that port. The strategy of Axis MTBs in the Adriatic also changed and from then on offensive operations such as ambushes, harbor forcing actions, and commando raids were authorized for German and Italian boats.

On the night of 23 August, during an attack on some units spotted by air reconnaissance anchored outside Ancona's breakwater, the two MS of the Decima MAS attacked the British Hunt class destroyer *Brocklesby*. A torpedo missed the ship and exploded against the mole

Between the end of August and October 1944 the Germans temporarily "retrieved" *MS 41*, provisionally renaming her *SA 4* but retaining the Italian crew and flag. The idea was to use her as a transport for their small and unseaworthy Linsen explosive motor boats. In the meanwhile, an action took place on the night of 6 September 1944 off the coast of Rimini between *MS 75* and three British motor torpedo boats. The Italian boat withdrew without consequences while *MTB 289* and *298* reported some damage.

33. *A Marina Repubblicana patrol boat at Venice 1944. (Storia Militare)*

An attempt by *SA 4* to force Ancona on the night of 15 September failed because the Linsen assigned to support the Italian and German swimmers capsized at the harbor mouth. A subsequent mission on the 18th of that same month also aborted, this time, because of British vigilance.

On the night of 11 November the recently returned *MS 41* hit a mine while trying to rescue the German *S 33* which had grounded off Ravenna.

This was a blow as the increasingly poor relations with the Germans in the politically sensitive Adriatic area had delayed the scheduled return to the Republican Navy of *MAS 550* and *554*. The only increase in the tiny nucleus of the Decima MAS's surface force in the Adriatic, therefore, consisted of two SMA in poor condition obtained by a private initiative of Lieutenant Sergio Nesi in February 1945. They were to be the core of a never constituted Italian Istrian flotilla of assault craft. Repaired, refitted, and renamed by Nesi *K 1* and *K 2*, the boats entered service in early April.

34. *Trials of a new CB submarine at Pola, winter 1944-1945. (Storia Militare)*

Units of the Decima MAS also served in a coast defense role. On 3 December 1944 a strong British force of four destroyers, four of the large "D" class MTBs and three LCGs (Landing Craft Gun, armed with a pair of 4.7-inch weapons) and six other craft attacked Lussinpiccolo in the upper Adriatic on Lussino (Losinj) Island. Decima MAS personnel manned the nearby 152-mm battery on Monte Asino and took the British raiders under fire. In a five hour action the destroyer *Wilton* and *MTB 633* sustained light damage while the Italians captured some of the Partisans supporting the British artillery observation party that had been landed on the island the night before. This action, in which both sides claimed victory, was noteworthy not because of its limited material effects or the participation of Decima MAS personnel, but as another indication of the psychological impact of the small attack units as one of the reasons for the whole affair was to strike at "human torpedoes" and/or "explosive motor boats" the British believed were based at coves in the vicinity.

In fact, the major function of the battery was to help ensure the continuation of the vital nocturnal coastal traffic in coal along the Istrian peninsula and the northern Italy. This traffic, which averaged 100,000 tons a month, was conducted by sailing vessels escorted mostly by the Marina Repubblicana's last minesweepers, gunboats, and patrol vessels under the daytime coverage of Italian manned shore batteries. It included coal from the mines of Arsa which was reserved for civilian use and, during the terrible

35. *Venice May 1944 Italian and German sailors. (Storia Militare)*

winter of 1944/45, made a life or death difference for many. This task became increasingly difficult as the British considered that sea lane as their most important target in the Adriatic from the autumn of 1944.

On 9 March, 1945 a prompt Italian reaction frustrated another raid against Lussino by a British party carried in three motor launches.

Meanwhile, on January 10, 1945, *MS 75* and four similar German units scored a coup de main with a landing on the island of Mljet in the war of pinpricks that the two sides were fighting in that corner of Europe during the conflict's final months. This action was followed by landings of agents along the Italian coast and Yugoslav by Decima MAS units. By this point a shortage of gasoline compelled the Axis fast coastal forces to curtail their offensive operations leaving most of the patrolling to the three or four diesel-fueled S-Boats available. The Kriegsmarine's Adriatic leadership continued, however, its aggressive posture, even conducting some harbor-forcing missions, the most successful being on the night of 24 February when five MTM explosive boats entered Spalato (Split) harbor and damaged the British cruiser *Delhi* and destroyed a landing craft.

The Decima MAS attempted one last mission against Ancona on 14 April with its two SMA. This did not produce results in part due to an accident which prevented *K1* from attacking the British destroyer *Avon Vale* seen leaving that port. The attempt ended with scuttling of the two units.

36. *Venice, July 1944. Italo-German crew of a 6-inch battery. (Uniformi e Armi)*

On 29 April, following the arrival in Venice of the first Italian and British advance parties, *MS 75* was delivered to the Regia Marina along with some auxiliary ships (notably the training ship *Marco Polo*, the tug *Chirone*, and six patrol boats engaged in surveillance tasks) and more than 50,000 GRT of merchant shipping. These surrenders accorded with Borghese's orders given on 26 April. The head of the Decima MAS was now interested in preserving materials for Italy in anticipation of a future conflict with Belgrade or even between the Soviets and Western Allies. The same principal was applied to the midget submarines *CM 1* and *CB 19*, which arrived in Venice from Pola on 2 May sailing surfaced with most of the personnel of the small submarine flotilla crowded aboard.

On that same day a dozen German vessels including the last seven S-boats loaded with German troops escaping from Trieste surrendered to a squadron of Royal Navy MTBs at the mouth of the Tagliamento River. The landing craft *F 944 DM*, *F 1045 DM*, *F 1046 DM*, *F 1155 D*, and *F 1191 D* rounded up at Ancona were ceded to the Regia Marina as part of its booty.

Chapter 9 Dragon's teeth

On January 1945, after the failure of the Battle of the Bulge, Prince Borghese began to seriously consider the fact that surrendering was one of the soldiering profession's many aspects. He had first conceived a soft passage of power in September 1944, when the end of the war in Italy seemed eminent. The scheme was the same the next spring: an agreement with the resistance's more moderate elements like the Catholics and liberals, and also with America's embryonic spy service, the OSS, courtesy of carefully maintained links with the Regia Marina. Borghese had a list of priorities: to save his people from retribution, particularly by the partisans; to seal his force's reputation by conducting a last Valkyarian general sortie before scuttling the surviving attack craft; and to secure the honors of war and have an ordered passage of powers to the winners according to the classic form.

There were other priorities as well, first among all the defense of Italy's eastern frontier against Tito's army. The Prince was aware, however, that the two brigades groups of the Decima MAS Division were well integrated into the German order of battle along the Gothic line and lacked mobility. On 21 April the U.S. 10th Mountain Division forced the last Appennini strongholds and entered Bologna allowing the Allied armies to begin deluging the Po River valley and Borghese ordered his troops to make for Trieste to support there the local Italian garrisons (some scattered Decima MAS territorial companies included). However, this was a race between men on foot and the Allies in trucks, half-tracks, and tanks and the final could be only the surrender, on 29 April 1945, of the I Gruppo at Padova to a platoon of the 12th

37. *A Servizio Ausiliario Femminile (Female Auxiliary Service) poster of the Decima MAS. (Uniformi e Armi)*

Royal Lancers and on 30 April of the II Gruppo to the U.S. Army's 88th Infantry Division at Schio and Marostica. In both cases the honors of war were granted.

These gentlemanly final acts, so important to the Italian Quixotic sense of drama and history, were favored by the desire to avoid, on both sides, useless deaths during the final days of that long, bloody war. Other units of the Decima MAS surrendered to the Americans at, Montorfano, Novara, Montecchio, and Genoa between the 27th and 30th. After nine days of local truce the troops in Venice, concentrated on the eastern island of Sant'Elena, surrendered on 7 May 1945.

The 200 strong Turin Company preferred to stay there rather than following the Italian and German army garrisons which left on 26 April for Milan, according to their orders. It was a bad choice as a three day siege by the partisans exhausted the Turin Company's munitions. Before the enemy's final assault, on 30 April, most of the defenders escaped through a tunnel, but about seventy (including women) were seized and killed.

The Decima's units at Cherso Island, Fiume, Trieste, and Pola fought alongside the Italian and German units there until the final surrender of that last town on 6 May. Many died but some prisoners came home in spring 1947.

38. *A 1945 recruiting poster for the Decima MAS. By now a red X was all the text necessary. (Enrico Cernuschi)*

Borghese's final acts played out in Milan in April 1945 where he had a force of about seven hundred men and some women within a city of a half million. The Prince realized that the city's four-thousand-strong German garrison, locked in their barracks, had negotiated a separate truce with the partisans. This bargain went into effect early on the afternoon of 25 April and from that moment the Germans limited their activity to self-defense without concern for their allies. Being aware he could only trust his men, Borghese played a complex game with the partisans, the Germans, and the Allies with the final goal being his aforementioned priorities. On 26 April just before dawn the Decima MAS check points that protected Borghese's command post in the centrally located Milanese barrack of Piazzale Fiume easily repulsed a halfhearted attack by Guardia di Finanza troops. This was a small, but significant event as the guards had just openly switched aides and easily seized that morning, with a force of little more than four hundred men, the prefecture, radio station, and city hall.

As that small force totaled nearly its entire organized military strength in Milan, the resistance leaders soon accepted a truce with the Decima MAS. Borghese, however, being well aware the partisans from the country were much more dangerous decided not to waste any time for his personnel's sake. By the afternoon of the 26th the Decima MAS in Milan demobilized and after a final ceremony everyone was allowed to go home with a pass. At 1900 Borghese himself sortied last with his aid de camp. In the confusion following the liberation no one noticed his uniform and he easily reached a safe house. On 12 May, fourteen days after the first US Army troops entered Milan, he traveled to Rome in a jeep with an OSS party and was later interned in the Cinecittà POW camp. There, with the Regia Marina's blessing, he discussed an American proposal to the Decima MAS underwater team in Venice to train U.S. Navy personnel in anticipation of a frogman attack against the last Japanese warships afloat in the home islands--a project the Italian navy had begun to study in 1944 with American support.

Borghese remained a prisoner until February 1949. By that time the majority of his men had reenlisted in the Italian navy reserve (and some specialists in the active service with the restriction that their career would stop at the rank of captain). Some combatant vessels also survived. *MS 75*, the midget submarines *CM 1* and *CB 19*, the school ship *Marco Polo*, and some small auxiliary ships. Of the Tyrrhenian naval forces only *MAS 525*, scuttled at Genoa on 24 April 1945 before being commissioned by the Marina Repubblicana, could be raised, repaired and commissioned again in 1948.

39. *The Mascottina, Mussolini's personal motor boat since 1938. After the armistice it was transferred from Rome to Lake Garda and later during the spring of 1945, to Lake Como to deceive the many parties who were looking for the Italian dictator in April 1945. The boat was lost in an accident on 4 May 1946. Gina Mussolini, the Duce's daughter-in-law who had accepted the invitation of two British officers to take a joy ride, died in the accident. (Enrico Cernuschi)*

Chapter 10. A Forgotten War

As participants in the three distinct Mediterranean naval campaigns fought in the Western Mediterranean, Adriatic, and Aegean seas between 9 September 1943 and 8 May 1945, the logistic and operational contributions of more than ten thousand Italian sailors ashore and afloat *Im Diest der Deutsche Wehrmacht*, in the service of the German armed forces, was inconspicuous but decisive, considering that German navy personnel in this sea never exceeded thirteen thousand men between 1944 and 1945. Likewise, the nearly as many sailors serving in the Republican navy's ranks played a significant role.

In this latter group there were few sea-going personnel engaged in offensive operations--a few hundred volunteers only--but this allowed the Decima MAS to select the best men available and its attack craft crews obtained results that reflected their quality. The Marina nera's role was less glamorous, but its escorts, minesweepers, patrol boats, support vessels, coastal batteries, and shore services in Italy, in the Balkans and elsewhere likewise played a crucial role in that last season of the war at sea, facing high human and material costs without the satisfaction of being able to adequately respond to enemy attack. In this context, the contributions of the Italian merchant marine to the Axis effort should also be noted.

The importance of the Italian contribution can be gauged by considering the surface encounters fought in the Mediterranean Sea after the armistice of 8 September 1943. The records suggest that there were at least 311 actions involving cruisers, destroyers, escort, and coastal forces (plus seven harbor-forcing actions on both sides). This number cannot be considered final as the various sources do not coincide and many of the original documents were lost or are still waiting to be surveyed; however, according to the logic of big numbers, it allows a sound base for statistical analysis.

Excluding the sixteen naval actions fought between the Germans and the Italians between 9 and 13 September 1943 (twelve in the Western Mediterranean and four in the Aegean Sea) as a consequence of the armistice and the fifteen Adriatic clashes and three Aegean actions between Axis ships (fourteen by the Germans and four by the Italian Marina Repubblicana) against Tito's partisans and SOE parties, the totals of the encounters become:

Western Mediterranean	128
Adriatic Sea	98
Aegean Sea	54

These 280 actions can be classified by offensive missions:

Area	Allied	German	Italian Axis
W. Med	86	21	21
Adriatic	92	3	3
Aegean	54	0	0

Of the Allied attacks 165, almost all directed against enemy traffic, were made by coastal forces and the remaining sixty-seven by cruisers and/or destroyers (about a third by the USN navy, alone or with the participation of Royal Navy coastal forces and the remainder by the British, except for six Italian co-belligerency and five French offensive encounters included in the total). All of the Axis actions were carried out by MTBs or attack craft. These numbers suggest several conclusions:

First, the Axis surface offensive activity in the Mediterranean after the 8 September 1943 armistice was a 50-50 affair between the Kriegsmarine and the Decima Flottiglia MAS where the more experienced Italians quickly dictated the doctrine, tactic and strategy despite some eccentric German underwater endeavors.

Second, the Axis campaign for the defense of its sea lanes was successful, despite the huge enemy superiority at sea and in the air. The traffic with Spain, of great importance to Italian industry and economy, suffered losses of about 10 percent, but continued regularly until the Allied landing in Provence.[39] The Adriatic traffic achieved similar results. The Axis troops there needed 100,000 tons of seaborne supplies a month because rail and land transport networks were inadequate (or threatened by Partisan activities). This tonnage was successfully delivered until the final retreat in November 1944. In the opposite direction a mosquito armada of small ships, mainly Italian, carried at

---

[39] According to Angelo Tarchi, the Saló Republic's economic minister. See Tarchi, *Test Dure*, 119-21.

night, under the protection of escort forces, minefields and shore batteries a flow of Albanian crude oil and chrome, Greek nickel, and Montenegrine bauxite for the Reich suffering troublesome, but never decisive losses from Allied destroyers and MTBs. The story was the same in the case of Arsa coal for Italian ovens in 1944-1945, the only difference being that Marina Repubblicana ships and shore batteries were the lone participants in an obscure but vital campaign. The sea communications along the French, Greek, Italian and Aegean coastlines was maintained until the last harbor fell conquered from the land and not from the sea.

This full picture allows one to appreciate a final fundamental lesson: Kriegsmarine staff was right to concentrate its sparse assets, after 8 September 1943, to the protection of the coastal traffic, from Spain to the Dardanelles. From November 1942 the Wehrmacht's task in the Mediterranean was to endure giving the German army a chance in the east or in the west to obtain a Frederick-the-Great-miracle-victory. However, to be effective any guerrilla campaign must have an offensive sting, no matter how small. In such a campaign this component is too fragile to hazard the Mahanian decisive battle and must, in fact, be founded upon the use of expendable warships.

This decisive role of the Axis naval guerrilla campaign between the autumn of 1943 and spring 1945 was correctly understood and attained by Borghese and his men. MAS boats, like the S-boats in the Adriatic, had to be employed with relative care but the SMA and MTMs were truly expendable, despite their hand-picked crews. They were mobile, as they had efficient motorized support groups, and were small enough to be easily camouflaged avoiding in this way the threat of a direct air bombing attack. The excellent use of propaganda by Borghese and his management style complemented this correct strategy.

The Germans, after having so severely criticized the Regia Marina's priorities regarding the defense of the sea lanes during the first three years of the Mediterranean war, adopted the same approach after the 8 September 1943 armistice and copied, with little success, Borghese's offensive methods during the last two years of war. It could be considered a case of poetic justice.

The global repercussions of this strategy are suggested by the vicissitudes of the British Eastern Fleet. After the 8 September 1943 armistice the British War Cabinet and the Admiralty anticipated a good harvest in the Indian

Ocean transferring Admiral Somerville's Eastern Fleet from the confined waters of Mombasa to Ceylon. In the meanwhile they began replacing Somerville's scrap iron vessels with four efficient battleships and a modern carrier from the Mediterranean and a division of adequate cruisers. However, it was still necessary to ask for American help in the form of the carrier *Saratoga* and some destroyers as the new battle fleet, when concentrated south of Colombo on 27 March 1944, had only seven destroyers to escort nearly as many capital ships. At that same time the Royal Navy had nearly sixty destroyers and, much more importantly, plenty of experienced and tested personnel in the Mediterranean on board the cruisers, destroyers, motor torpedo and motor gun boats, and submarines searching for and painstakingly pursuing swarms of Axis auxiliaries, landing craft, and steamers, and avoiding night ambuscades off Anzio, Imperia or Ancona by tiny motor boats armed with small torpedoes and bombs.

The next year the destroyer situation of the Eastern Fleet improved with thirty units available, but they were outnumbered by the forty-four still operating in the Mediterranean, plus eight Greek units borrowed from Britain. Thus, the greater situation was little changed causing what Correlli Barnett labeled an "operational doldrums."[40] The anticipated political and strategic harvest promised by the Italian armistice had failed.

---

[40] **Barnett**, *Engage the Enemy More Closely*, 878.

Appendix I. Organization of the Marina Repubblicana

Secretary of the Navy

Antono Legnani: 23 September 1943 - 19 October 1943
Ferruccio Ferrini: 26 October 1943 - 14 February 1944
Giuseppe Sparzani: 16 February 1944 - 26 February 1945
Bruno Gemelli: 26 February 1945 - 26 April 1945

Chief of Staff

Antonio Legnani: 23 September 1943 - 19 October 1943
Giuseppe Sparzani: 28 October 1943 - 26 February. 1945
Junio Valerio Borghese: 26 February 1945 - 26 April 1945

Naval Organization

Secretary of the Navy with separate departments for
- Personnel
- Administration
- Provost
- Sanitary Corps
- Constructions
- Weapons
- Electronics
- German Liaison
- Communications
- Motor and Transportation
- Naval Academy
- Survey service
- Stato Maggiore (Staff)
- Surface vessels inspectorate
- Submarine inspectorate
- Attack craft inspectorate
- Anti-submarine inspectorate

Naval infantry
Intelligence
MARICOSER (Comando Zona Servizi Marina) harbor and coastal services, arsenals, shore batteries, signaling

Regional Commands

Distaccamento Marina versante Tirrenico (Tyrrhenian Sea)
Comando Marina versante Adriatico (Adriatic Sea)
Comando Marina regioni Centrali (Latium, Tuscany and Abruzzi)

Operational Commands

Comando operativo Marina Tirreno (Genoa)
Squadriglia MAS "Castagnacci"
Base Operativa Sud, then Base Operativa Ovest
Gruppo Operativo Gamma
Gruppo Operativo S.S.B.
Squadriglia Sommergibili CA
Squadriglia Sommergibili in allestimento
Base Collegamento con l'Italia occupata (clandestine operations)
ANTISOM flotilla
Comando operativo Marina Adriatico
Squadriglia Motosiluranti
Squadriglia Sommergibili CB e CM
Gruppo ANTISOM Adriatico
Base Operativa Est

Training

Gruppo "Todaro" Scuola Mezzi d'assalto di superficie
Scuola Sommozzatori "Licio Visintin"

Foreign Commands

Base Atlantica (Bordeaux and Saint Nazaire) Shore batteries and naval infantry

Germany One smoke screen chemical battalion
Dalmatia (shore batteries at Sebenico)
Black Sea (Costanza) midget submarines
Dodecanneso (Rhodes) Shore batteries
Crete (Suda) Shore batteries
China (Tianjin) naval infantry

Appendix II. Armed Warships and Auxiliary Vessels of the Marina Repubblicana

Legend: * not actually commissioned by the Marina Repubblicana
A: Adriatic Sea
T: Tyrrhenian Sea
E: Aegean Sea
BS: Black Sea

Fast coastal forces

MAS 430 (A) Ceded to the Kriegsmarine by late November 1943. Damaged in an air raid on 6 December 1943 at Sebenico and paid off.

MAS 431 (A) Lost with no survivors between Zara and Sebenico by unknown causes in November 1943.

MAS 433 (A) Mutinied on 19 November 1943 and rejoined the Regia Marina.

MAS 502 (T) Commissioned February 1944. Damaged by a German army battery off Anzio on 5 March 1944 and stranded at Follonica. Recovered and damaged again while under tow on 12 April 1944 by a German KT transport which rammed the boat; stranded again at Follonica and later destroyed there with scuttling charges.

MAS 504 (T) Commissioned March 1944. Rammed and sunk by the destroyer HMS *Grenville* off Anzio on 25 March 1944.

MAS 505 (T) A Regia Marina boat whose crew mutinied on 10 April 1944 and joined the Germans. Commissioned by the Kriegsmarine as *SA 19*. Ceded to the Marina Repubblicana autumn 1944. Scuttled at Porto Maurizio 24 April 1945.

MAS 522 (E) A Regia Marina craft which mutinied on 18 September 1943. Ceded to the Kriegsmarine on 15 November 1943. Sunk by British aircraft on 4 December 1943 off Makrosinos Island.

MAS 531 (T) Commissioned February 1944. Sunk on 11 December 1944 by the French submarine chaser *Sabre*.

MAS 544 (T) Commissioned March 1944. Sunk in an USAAF raid on Genoa on 1 September 1944.

40. MAS 561 *at Lerici 1944. (Storia Militare)*

MAS 553 (T) Commissioned January 1945. Scuttled at Porto Maurizio on 24 April 1945.

MAS 556 (T) Commissioned February 1944. Scuttled at Porto Maurizio on 24 April 1945.

MAS 557 (T) Commissioned March 1944. Damaged 30 April 1944 after an encounter with the Allied forces off Anzio. Stranded at Ostia and destroyed there by scuttling charges.

MAS 561 (T) Commissioned March 1944. Sunk 23 April 1945 by USN PT boats.

MAS 562 (T) Commissioned February 1944. Captured by USN PT boats on 30 June 1944 and returned to the Regia Marina the next month. Recommissioned September 1944.

MS 41 (A) Commissioned February 1944. Mined 27 September 1944.

MS 75 (A) Commissioned February 1944. Surrendered at Venice 29 April 1945.

From 11 October 1943 there was a program to commission in the Adriatic Sea the MTBs *MS 16** and *34** (to be transferred from the Tyrrhenian Sea via the Po River) and *MAS 550** and *554**, under refit at Monfalcone and Venice respectively. After the loss of *MS 16* in a bomber raid at Genoa on January 1944 this plan was cancelled and the material recovered from these MTBs was used to complete a new batch of MTBs of the same type named by the Germans *S 621-628* which had been put on the slip in

August 1943. On April 1944 the Kriegsmarine briefly rearmed the two Adriatic MAS boats for patrol duties.

MAS 525*, *549*, *551* and *558*, all in the Tyrrhenian Sea, were to have been commissioned by the Marina Repubblicana, but the Germans retained the last three commissioning them in July 1944 as *SA 12*, *13*, and *15*. *MAS 525* was scuttled at Genoa on 24 April 1945 before completing.

MA/SB

RA 252 (former *VAS 305*) 92 t (T) Commissioned May 1944. Scuttled at Genoa 24 April 1945.

RA 253 (former *VAS 307*) 92 t (T) Commissioned September 1944. Scuttled at Genoa 24 April 1945.

RA 263 (former *VAS 308*) 92 t (T) Commissioned 16 May 1944. Scuttled at Genoa 24 April 1945.

Motor Launches

MV 30 (A) Former *ML 30* of the Regia Guardia di Finanza. Scuttled at Venice 29 April 1945.

MV 32 (A) as *MV 30*.

MV 34 (T) as *MV 30* except scuttled at Genoa on 24 April 1945.

The Decima MAS also armed at least ten MTSM and twenty five MTSMA. (Usually shortened to SMA). There were about a dozen of these torpedo armed attack craft available at any given time between December 1943 and April 1945.

Four MTRs, a smaller explosive boat designed to be carried by a submarine inside the cylinders used for human torpedoes, were commissioned.

Motor boats

serving as attack craft and commando transports
MTL 476 (T).
MTL 571 (T) Commissioned January 1945.
MCN 567 (T).
All scuttled 23 April 1945 at Spezia.

On 8 September 1943 the Picchiotti yard at Limite d'Arno was building five 18 meter long wooden fast motor boats. It proposed to complete them as MTBs armed with one 450-mm torpedo and one 20 mm MG and named *MAS PL 1-5*. The Decima MAS command accepted the program but the boats were not completed before the Allied conquest of Tuscany in August 1944.

Twelve 56-ton wooden antiaircraft patrol boats armed with 37 and 20-mm guns had been ordered by the Regia Marina in 1943 at the Prometeo yards of Genoa. The Marina Repubblicana took over the contract, but none were delivered before the war's end.

The Marina Repubblicana also armed on Lake Garda three motor boats, one of them Mussolini's personal craft named *Mascottina*. She was later transferred in 1945 to Lake Maggiore as a decoy to cover the dictator's proposed plan to flee to Switzerland.

The deluxe motor yacht of Giuseppe Volpi, a Venetian industrialist, was pressed in service by the Decima MAS in the summer of 1944 to ferry saboteur squads behind the enemy lines in the Adriatic Sea. The vessel was lost on her first mission to unknown causes.

Submarines

Beilul * (A) Returned to the Marina Repubblicana October 1943. Sunk in an USAAF raid in 25 May 1944 at Monfalcone just before recommissioning. Recovered, but not repaired. Scuttled again 1 May 1945.

Aradam* (T) Returned to the Marina Repubblicana October 1943. Seized by the Germans 18 August 1944 when nearing end of refit. Sunk at Genoa in an USAAF raid 4 September 1944.

Murena* (T) Scuttled at Spezia 9 September 1943. Raised by the Decima MAS and sent to Genoa for refit. Seriously damaged in an USAAF raid on 4 September 1944. Scuttled 23 April 1945.

Sparide* (T) As *Murena*. Sunk in an USAAF raid on Genoa 4 September 1944.

Grongo* (T) She had not yet been commissioned by the Regia Marina on 8 September 1943. Fate as *Sparide*.

Midget submarines

CB 1 (BS) On 19 December 1943 the boat's crew asked to be interned by the Romanian government and the midget, worn out after almost three years of war in the Mediterranean and Black Sea, remained immobilized. On 30 January 1944 the boat was formally given to the Marina Repubblicana. At first the idea was to send a new CB flotilla from Italy. However, losses caused by a USAAF raid against Pola on 9 January 1944 induced staff to send personnel to Costanza in April 1944 with the purpose of cannibalizing the five Black Sea boats to get *CB 1*, *3* and *6* serviceable (even if only *CB 3* was actually recommissioned). *CB 1*, reduced to a hulk, was abandoned on 25 August 1944 after the declaration of the Romanian armistice.

CB 2 (BS) as *CB 1*.

CB 3 (BS) Recommissioned on June 1944. On 25 August 1944 scuttled off Costanza.

CB 4 (BS) as *CB 1*.

CB 6 (BS) as *CB 1*.

CA 2 (T) Recovered autumn 1943 by the Decima MAS. Paid off spring 1944.

CA 3 (T) Recovered autumn 1943 by the Decima MAS. Served as an ASW training boat until August 1944 and then paid off.

CA 4 (T) Recovered by the Decima MAS like *CA 2* and *3* and transferred by the Kriegsmarine to Germany in 1944 for study in the development of their midget type XXVII B Seehund.

CB 7 (A) Previously damaged by an internal explosion on 14 July 1943. Repaired autumn 1943. Paid off after serious damage suffered in the USAAF raid against Pola on 9 January 1944 and cannibalized for parts.

CB 13 (A) Commissioned November 1943. Sunk in a bomber raid against Pola on 23 March 1945.

CB 14 (A) Commissioned December 1943. Destroyed in an USAAF raid against Pola on 9 January 1944.

CB 15 (A) as *CB 14*.

41. *The submarine* CM 1 *January 1945. (Storia Militare)*

CB 16 (A) Commissioned December 1943. On 1 October 1944 the crew mutinied killing the commander. The boat stranded at Senigallia and was a total loss.

CB 17 (A) Commissioned 30 September 1944. Sunk by an aircraft south of Cattolica 2 April 1945.

CB 18 (A) Commissioned 20 October 1944. Scuttled at Pola 2 May 1945.

CB 19 (A) Commissioned 23 September 1944. Surrendered at Venice 2 May 1945.

CB 20 (A) Commissioned 31 October 1944. Damaged 2 May 1945 at Pola by the explosion of two mines. Recovered postwar by the Yugoslavian navy and named *Malisan*.

CB 21 (A) Commissioned 31 December 1944. Sunk in the Fasana Channel after a collision with a German landing craft 29 April 1945.

CB 22 (A) Commissioned February 1945. Sunk by British aircraft at Lussinpiccolo 11 March 1945.

CB 23*, 24*, 25* and *26** (A), were delivered December 1944--April 1945 from the Caproni factory to be fitted at Grignano, Venice, and Trieste by the Decima MAS. They were never completed. *CB 23* and *24*, almost ready, were scuttled at Grignano (Miramare – Trieste) 2 May 1945; *CB 23* was scuttled at Venice 28 April 1945 and *CB 26* at Trieste 2 May 1945.

The Marina Repubblicana ordered a further series of CB boats (*27-66*) on 30 June 1944 and 30 September 1944 but none were laid down.

CM 1 (A) Commissioned 5 January 1945. Surrendered 2 May at Venice.

CM 2* (A) Heavily damaged in an air raid at Monfalcone on 25 May 1944 and never commissioned. Scuttled 2 May 1945.

Three similar boats (*CC 1, 2,* and *3*), ordered originally by the Regia Marina, were confirmed by the Marina Repubblicana on 5 October 1943. On 22 December 1944 the contract for the three boats was cancelled when they were respectively 60, 57 and 38 percent complete as precedence was given to an order for a hundred Siebel ferries for the German army.

Experimental boats

This category includes the prototype of the Bussei hydrofoil, transferred to Germany in 1944; the *K3*, a 19.6 meter submersible motor boat, completed and tested by the Germans (with an Italian crew) at Spezia in autumn 1944 and scuttled there on 23 April 1945; two Caproni 6-ton 25 knot single engine type submarines ordered early 1943, but still building on April 1945, which were requisitioned by the USN on May 1945 and the single engined private venture 5-ton submarine *Delfino*, ordered October 1943 and completed at Lecco, on Lake Como, the next year for a series of trials. The U. S. Navy sized the boat postwar.

In October 1943 The Marina Repubblicana ordered fifty 15.5 meter 50 knot Bussei hydrofoils armed with two 450-mm torpedoes and one 37-mm to be assembled near Verona and deployed by flotillas in the Tyrrhenian and Adriatic seas. The order was subsequently reduced to four and then, in January 1944, to two hydrofoils, *BUS 1* and *2* but none completed before the war's end.

Torpedo Boats

T 7 (A) Ceded to the German Navy in late November 1943 when she was worn out. Recommissioned after an eight month refit under the German flag with a Croat crew as *TA 34* and sunk by British MTBs on 24 June 1944.

Pilo (A) Mutinied and, with the tug *Porto Conte*, rejoined the Regia Marina on 26 September 1943.

Missori (A) Commissioned by the Germans after 6 October 1943.

The fast rescue tug *Proteo*, still on the slip at Ancona on 8 September 1943, was to be armed by the Marina Repubblicana as an escort ship under the name of *Perseo*. She was towed to Trieste in 1944 and scuttled there on 1 May 1945 before completing. She was later recovered by the Italian navy and commissioned in 1955 under her original name.

Destroyers and Cruisers

Early October 1943 programs envisaged the recovery and recommission by the Marina Repubblicana of the destroyer *Maestrale**, the torpedo boat *Ghibi** and the corvettes *FR 51** and *FR 52,** all in the Tyrrhenian Sea. In January 1944, however, the Germans cancelled this program.

The hulks of the cruisers *Etna** and *Vesuvio**, still under construction at Trieste on 8 September 1943 and stripped by the Germans after the armistice, were formally returned to the Marina Repubblicana in September 1944 with the intent to save the hulls for postwar completion. They were both scuttled on 1 May 1945.

Auxiliary cruisers

Arborea (A) 4,959 GRT two 4.7-inch guns. Commissioned by the Germans in early October 1943 at Trieste. Seriously damaged in an Allied raid at Sebenico on 12 January 1944 and sunk five days later.

Pola (A) 451 GRT. Mutinied and rejoined the Regia Marina on 21 September 1943.

Rovigno (A) 451 GRT Sunk by British MTBs in Valona Bay on 22 September 1943.

Armed transports

Italia (A) 5,203 GRT. Sunk by bombers 6 July 1944 at Arsa in the Istria peninsula.

Goffredo Mameli (A) 4,338 GRT. Sunk by bombers at Muggia (Trieste) 14 November 1944.

Marco (A) 1,487 GRT sunk by bombers at Gravosa in Dalmatia, 31 October 1943.

Nazario Sauro (A) 109 GRT, one 6-pdr. Sunk in Quarnaro Roads on 31 December 1943, cause unknown.

San Giorgio (A) 364 GRT, one 6-pdr. Wrecked 12 February 1944 off the Po Delta.

San Salomone (A) one 6-pdr. Surrendered at Venice 29 April 1945.

Scarpanto (A) 498 GRT, one 6-pdr. Sunk by bombers at Arsa 5 March 1945.

Castelnuovo (A) One 6-pdr. Surrendered at Venice 29 April 1945.

Medea (A) One 6-pdr. as *Castelnuovo*.

Madera (A) One 6-pdr. as *Castelnuovo*.

Armed Trawlers

Levrera (A) Sunk 1944 in Dalmatia.

Lido (A) Sunk by bombers at Trieste 21 March 1945.

Gallipoli (E) Taken over by the Germans at the Piraeus, 15 November 1943.

Otranto (E) as *Gallipoli*.

42. *The auxiliary sub chaser* CS 12 Equa *at Spezia. (Storia Militare)*

Auxiliary sub chasers

La Santa Maria (T) A former motorsailer used as an antisubmarine school ship until 8 September 1943. Reclassified autumn 1944 as *CS* (Cacciasommergibile) *14*. Scuttled at Spezia 23 April 1945.

AS 2 (*Saba*) (A) A 42 ton custom guard motor boat armed before 8 September 1943 as an auxiliary sub chaser and lost off Dalmatia in 1944.

AS 10 (*Millemiglia IV*) (T) A motor boat armed with 13.2 mm machineguns and used as a patrol boat at Spezia by the ANTISOM flotilla. Scuttled at Spezia 23 April 1945.

AS 49 (*Nioi*) (E) A 61 ton custom guard motor boat with a mixed German and Italian crew sunk 29 October 1943 by the British submarine *Unsparing* off Stampalia while rescuing survivors from the German steamer *Ingeborg* torpedoed by that same boat three hours earlier.

AS 103 (*Capodistria*) (T) A 67 ton tug used as sub chaser and reclassified *CS 11*. Sunk by USAAF bombers at Genoa 4 September 1944.

AS 105 (*Equa*) (T) A 243 GRT motor ship. Reclassified *CS 12*. Rammed and sunk by a German vessel off Spezia on 10 June 1944.

AS 107 (*Antonio Landi*) (T) A former fishing vessel. Sunk by USAAF bombers at Genoa 1 September 1944.

AS 108 (*Nettuno II*) (T) A former fishing vessel.

AS 126 (*MB 25*) (A) A custom guard motor boat recovered by the Regia Marina at Venice on 29 April 1945.

AS 134 (*Salvore*) (A) A 167 GRT steamer.

AS 143 (*Alba Seconda*) (A) A former fishing vessel.

Meta (T) A former small hospital ship twin of *Equa* commissioned after 8 September by the Marina Repubblicana as *CS 13*. Scuttled at Spezia on 19 April 1945 and recovered postwar.

Auxiliary patrol boats

MEN 101 (T) A motor barge used as a small sub chaser at Spezia like the *Millemiglia IV*. Scuttled at Spezia 23 April 1945.

NG 105 (T) Like *MEN 101*. Scuttled at Spezia 23 April 1945.

Armed Motor Fishery Vessels

Sant'Eufemia (A) Armed by late September 1943 by volunteers from Zara with a single 47/32-mm anti-tank gun and some machineguns. Sunk by mistake 13 October 1943 by a German army battery.

San Simeone (A) as *Sant'Eufemia*. Disabled by a machinery defect 29 October 1943 and paid off.

Two small armed motor barges served at Zara in October 1943. They were paid off in November 1943.

Armed yacht

Cervo (A) A 33 GRT ex-Yugoslavian yacht named *Jadrica*. Wrecked off Grado 9 November 1944.

Small Minelayers

Albona (E) Taken over by the Kriegsmarine at the Piraeus 15 November 1943.

Rovigno (E) as *Albona*. She was a military vessel and not the auxiliary cruiser of the same name.

Harbor minelayers

Vallelunga (T) Sunk at Genoa by British bombers 28 May 1944.

Laurana (A) Sunk by British bombers at Trieste 20 February 1945.

These ships were manned by mixed German and Italian crews.

Minesweepers

RD 35 (E) Taken over by the Kriegsmarine at the Piraeus 15 November 1943.
RD 49 (T) Scuttled at Spezia 19 April 1945.
RD 62 (T) Scuttled at Genoa 24 April 1945.
Arbe (T) Scuttled at Genoa 24 April 1945.
RD 212 (T) A 100 ton wooden magnetic minesweeper completed and commissioned in 1944. Scuttled at Genoa on 24 April 1945.

Auxiliary minesweepers

Di Lio (A) Surrendered at Venice 29 April 1945.
Nicola Padre (A) 59 GRT. Sunk 7 January 1944 by the British destroyers *Jervis* and *Janus* off Porto San Giorgio.
San Giovanni (A) Surrendered at Venice 29 April 1945.
Traù (A) 160 GRT. Sunk by a mine on 31 January 1945 off the Tagliamento River.
Littorio (A) 32 GRT. Lost off San Benedetto del Tronto December 1943.
Adria (A) 45 GRT. Scuttled in Venice April 1945 and recovered postwar.
Balilla (A) 62 GRT. Sunk by bombers at Sebenico winter 1943.
Vittorio Bruno (A) Surrendered at Venice 29 April 1945.
Piave (E) Taken over by the Kriegsmarine at the Piraeus on 15 November 1943.
Antonio Chiesa (E) as *Piave*.

Trawler attack craft support ships

Pegaso (T) Repaired and recommissioned March 1944. Scuttled at Spezia 23 April 1945.
Cefalo (T) as *Pegaso*. Used later as a minesweeper. Sunk by bombers at Genoa 4 October 1944.

Landing Craft

MZ 703 II (T) Scuttled at Genoa on 24 April 1945.

MZ 736 (T) Scuttled at Genoa on 24 April 1945.

MZ 759 II (T) Sunk in Genoa by an USAAF raid on 1 September 1944.

MZ 704, *MZ 706*, *MZ 744*, *MZ 777*, *MZ 785*, and 799 were promised by the Germans in October 1943 but were instead commissioned by the Kriegsmarine.

Tugs

Chirone (A) 486 tons. Surrendered at Venice 29 April 1945 and re-named *San Giusto*.

Costante (A) 500 tons. Sunk 1944 in the Adriatic Sea.

Colonnello Pozzi (A) 100 tons. Scuttled in Venice April 1945 and recovered postwar.

Liscabianca (A) 106 tons. Sunk by Italian aircraft off Corfu 25 September 1943.

Marittimo (A) 342 tons. Sunk by aircraft off Pola June 1944.

Molara (A) 106 tons. Scuttled in the Ravenna channel November 1944.

Parenzo (A) 130 tons. Sunk by Allied aircraft off Premuda spring 1944.

Pertinace (A) 200 tons. Lost 1944.

Pianosa (A) 160 tons. Lost 1944 in Dalmatia.

Porto Conte (A) 230 tons. Mutinied with the torpedo boat *Pilo* on 26 September 1943 and rejoined the Regia Marina.

Rondine (A) 250 tons. Lost 1944.

Sant'Andrea (A) 192 tons. To Germany November 1944 and renamed *A. 27*.

Atlante (T) 362 tons. Scuttled at Genoa 24 April 1945. Recovered postwar.

Brava (T) 80 tons. Paid off and scrapped February 1945 at Spezia.

Capri (T) 112 tons. Scuttled at Spezia 19 April 1945.

Carbonara (T) 106 tons. As *Capri*.

Colosso (T) 385 tons. As *Capri*.

Licosa (T) 108 tons. Recovered Genoa 27 April 1945.

Linaro (T) 87 tons. As *Capri*.

Mesco (T) 87 tons. As *Capri*.

43. *The water carrier* Verbano. *In December 1943 the mother of Dr. Cernuschi was ferried from Zara to Venice in this ship. As* Verbano *was a tanker the one hundred plus civilian refugees crowded aboard had to remain on deck. It was raining when they left and so cold and windy during that long cruise that when a German field kitchen served soup, Dr. Cernuschi's mother, then 13, and her sisters, put the hot liquid on their almost frozen faces for the warmth instead of eating it. The next month the ship was torpedoed and later sunk after a fire. (Erminio Bagnasco collection)*

Palmaria (T) 232 tons. Scuttled at Genoa 24 April 1945.
Polifemo (T) 1,050 tons. As *Palmaria*.
Porto d'Anzio (T) 123 tons. As *Palmaria*
Porto Palo (T) 210 tons. As *Palmaria*
Porto Sdobba (T) 230 tons. As *Capri*.
Robusto (T) 395 tons. Sunk in Genoa by USAAF bombers 1 September 1944. Recovered postwar.
Sant'Antioco (T) 173 tons. Scuttled at Savona on 24 April 1945. Recovered postwar.

Santo Stefano (T) 123 tons. Recovered Genoa 27 April 1945. Mined 15 June 1945.

Senigallia (T) 187 tons. Sunk at Genoa by USAAF bombers 4 September 1944.

Taormina (T) 280 tons. As *Senigallia*

Tiravanti (T). 32 tons. As *Senigallia*

Titano (T) 971 tons. Lost 1944.

Torre Annunziata (T) 161 tons. As *Capri*.

Yard tugs

Adriatic: *N.7*, *N.8*, *N.10 II*, *N.12*, *N.16*, *N.18*, *N.21*, *N.75*, *N.91*, *N.95*, and *P.E.107* were lost during the retreat from Dalmatia in autumn 1944. *N.87* was sunk by USAAF bombers at Pola on 9 January 1944. *N.88* was sunk by Allied bombers at Fiume autumn 1944. *N.90* was mined off Capo Salvore February 1944. *N.4*, *N.5 II*, *N.78*, and *N.94* were recovered at Venice by the Regia Marina on 29 April 1945.

Tyrrhenian Sea: *N.5* was sunk by Allied aircraft 19 March 1944 at Portoferraio. *N.55* was scuttled at Marina di Massa August 1944. Both were recovered postwar. *N.9*, *N.10*, and *N.53* were scuttled at Spezia on 19 April 1945 and recovered after the war while *N.37* was destroyed at Spezia 19 April 1945 and never repaired.

Four small Rimorchatori Lagunari (Lagoon tugs) *RL 1*, *2*, *3*, and *9* served at Venice; *RL 2* was sunk by bombers 23 March 1945 while the other three were scuttled 28 April 1945 and recovered postwar.

Water carriers

Gondar ex- *Bormida* (T) 645 tons. Scuttled at Spezia 19 April 1945.

Cherca (A) 564 tons. Lost in Dalmatia in 1944.

Verbano (A) 592 tons. Damaged by the British *MTB 97* off Dalmatia on 23 January 1944 and sunk by aircraft at Dubrovnik 10 March 1944.

Tankers

Cocito (T) 1,182 tons. Scuttled at Savona 24 April 1945. Recovered in 1949

Volturno (T) 3,390 tons. Sunk by an USAAF raid on Genoa 1 September 1944.

Aniene (A) 254 tons. Sabotaged and seized by Yugoslavian troops at Spalato October 1944 and repaired May 1945.

Garda (A) 602 tons. Lost 1944 in Dalmatia.

Isarco (A) 269 tons. Surrendered at Venice 29 April 1945.

Stige (A) 1,364 tons. As *Isarco*.

Vippacco (A) 269 tons. As *Isarco*.

Pellice (A) 80 tons. Scuttled at Venice 29 April 1945.

Pescara (A) 72 tons. As *Pellice*.

The tankers *Dalmazia* (3,033 tons), *Leno* (280 tons), *Sprugola* (318 tons), *Stura* (126 tons), and *Timavo* (280 tons), all at Spezia, were not commissioned, but remained in maintenance. They were all scuttled on 19 April 1945 and recovered and commissioned by the Italian navy postwar.

Coastal transports

Betta N.5 475 tons. Sunk by an USAAF raid 1 September 1944.

Betta N.16 463 tons. Scuttled at Spezia on 19 April 1945.

Motorsailor training ship

Marco Polo (A). Ex-Yugoslavian *Jadran* seized April 1941. Used as pontoon in Venice 1944-1945. Recovered Venice 29 April 1945 and returned to Yugoslavia in 1946.

Submarine rescue self-propelled pontoons

Anteo (T) 1,253 t. Scuttled 23 April 1945 at Spezia and recovered postwar.

Two other pontoons, nicknamed Due ruote and Cicogna, former Austro-Hungarian auxiliary ships, were lost at Pola in an USAAF raid, 9 January 1944. In addition, the Marina Repubblicana commissioned dozens of pontoons, barges, and so forth for harbor and coastal duties in the Adriatic and Tyrrhenian seas.

Guardia di Finanza vessels

Guardia di Finanza (Custom Guard) vessels included steam picket boat *PB 30*, 8 tons; motor barges *MB 22* and *26*, 20-35 tons; and small motor launches *ML 12*, *16*, *18*, *19*, *20*, *26*, *32*, *35*, *37*, *54*, *56*, *62*, *63*, *65*, and *72* displacing from 4 to 22-tons and used as patrol boats at Venice and Trieste from September 1943 until April 1945. On 29 April 1945 they were recovered by the Regia Marina except for *MB 26* and *ML 19*, sunk 1945 by bombers in Venice and Trieste respectively.

The Guardia di Finanza (and, later, the Marina Repubblicana) armed *MB 14* at Durazzo. She was commissioned in November 1943 by the German navy. Serving in the Tyrrhenian Sea were the barges *MB 6*, sunk at San Remo 16 September 1944, and *MB 43*, *ML 24* and *P.B. 15*, all sunk in an USAAF raid against Genoa on 4 September 1944.

Hospital Ship

Virgilio (T) 11,718 GRT. Torpedoed by the British submarine *Uproar* off Fréjus 6 December 1943. Paid off at Toulon and scuttled there August 1944.

Armed self-propelled pontoons

GM 194 (T) Based at Savona and scuttled there 23 April 1945. She was armed with a single 15-inch gun after an accident in 1944 had disabled the second gun of the same caliber, and was manned by a mixed German and Italian crew.

GM 269 (T) Based at Genoa and armed with two 190/39-mm guns. Scuttled 24 April 1945.

GM 218 (A) In Venice. Armed with four 3-inch antiaircraft guns.

Target Ship

Tampico (A) A 4,957 GRT tanker at Venice used to train frogmen. Surrendered 29 April 1945.

Appendix III. Surface Actions fought by Marina Repubblicana Units

Actions in the Western Mediterranean from 9 September 1943 to 27 April 1945

Date	Area	Italian (Axis) Units	Allied Units	Results
22/23 Jan 44	Anzio	MTSM 206, 224 & 304	screen	+206, =304
20/21 Feb 44	Anzio	MTSM 206, 226 & 304	Gunboat(?)	=304
22/23 Feb 44	Anzio	MTSM 208, 208 & 236	PC 627	+236, =208
18/19 Mar 44	Anzio	MAS & 'SMA	PC 545	=MAS 531, +SMA 316
25-Mar-44	Anzio	MAS & 'SMA	PT & DD	=MTSM 206, +MAS 504
20/21 Apr 44	Anzio	3xSMA	screen	no results
30-Apr-44	Anzio	MAS 557 & 561	7xPT	=3xPT, +MAS 557
14-May-44	Anzio	SMA 308, 314 & 318	PC 626 & 627	+SMA 308. =PC 626, =PC 627
23/24 May 44	Anzio	SMA 306 & 318	PC 626	+SMA 318
29 May 44	Anzio	MAS 562	PT	=PT
29/30 Jun 44	Portoferraio	MAS 531 & 562	PT 306, 308 & 309	+MAS 562 (captured)
24/25 Aug 44	Cap Ferrat	2xSMA IT & 1xSMA GE	2xUS DD	no results
25/26 Aug 44	Villafranca	3xSMA	Le Fantasque	no results
7/8 Sep 44	C. Azzurra	3xSMA	PT 215 & 216	=1xSMA
910 Sep 44	C. Azzurra	IT & GE SMA	PT 206 & 214	+GE SMA
2/3 Oct 44	Ligurian S.	1xSMA	2xUS DD	no results
11 Dec 44	Ligurian S.	MAS 531, 556 & 561	Sabre	+MAS 531. =Sabre
17 Feb 45	Ligurian S.	1xSMA	PT	no results
15/16 Mar 45	Ligurian S.	MAS 505 & 556	Lansquenet	=Lansquenet
17 Apr 45	Ligurian S.	1xSMA & 6 MTM	Trombe	=Trombe
23/24 Apr 45	Ligurian S.	MAS 561	PT 305 & 307	+MAS 561

Actions in the Ionian and Adriatic Seas from 9 September 1943 to 2 May 1945

21/22 Sep 43	Valona	Shipping in port	*MTB 287, 290 & 295*	+AMC *Rovigno*. =*MTB 295*.
2 Oct 43	Canale di Zara	*San Simeone* & *Sant'Eufemia*	Partisan m/s	2xm/s captured
3 Oct 43	Canale di Zara	*San Simeone Sant'Eufemia* w/ 2 mb	Partisan m/s	2xm/s captured
5 Oct 43	Canale di Zara	*San Simeone Sant'Eufemia* w/ 1 mb	Partisan m/s	2xm/s captured
27 Oct 43	Canale di Zara	*San Simeone* w/ 2 mb	Partisan m/s	4x m/s captured
23 Aug 44	Ancona	*MS 41 & 75*	*Brocklesby*	no results
6/7 Sep 44	Rimini	*MS 75*	3x MTB	=*MTB 289 & 298*
14 Apr 45	Ancona	SMA *K1*	*Avon Vale*	no results

Harbor Forcing actions by Special Assault Craft from 9 September 1943 to 2 May 1945

14 Dec 44	Livorno	3xGamma, *SMA 510*		no results
23/24 Apr 45	Ajaccio	2xSMA IT & 1xSMA GE		no results
23/24 Apr 45	Cap d'Antibes	1xSMA GE & 2xMTM IT	*Lansquenet, CH 112 & 122 & Intermondia*	+1xSMA, 2xMTM. =*Intermondia*

Abbreviations: + sunk; = damaged; DD destroyer; DC corvette; PT patrol torpedo boat; MTB motor torpedo boat; MFV motor fishing vessel; PC patrol craft; s/v sail vessel; m/s motorsailor

Bibliography

Primary and Official Sources

Archivio Centrale dello Stato. A.C.S.F., titolo II, Busta 1, "L'8 settembre 1943 al Ministero della Marina."

Archives Dept. Marine, Chateau de Vincennes, Service historique de la Defense, Archives Dept. Marine. *Le Fantasque* Dossier TTY 296 – Journal de bord n°4/1944 (28/7-28/9) 4 Division.

---. "Flank Force Compte-rendu Jaujard a FONAM del 15/2 nave *Le – Fortuné*."

---. "Compte-rendu Jaujard a FONAM de l'ensemblre des opérations de navires *Cimeterre* et *CH 105*, 17-18/4/45."

---. "Flank Force, Groupe de Surveillance – Compte-rendu de l'ensemblre des opérations de la nuit du 23 au 24 avril 1945. 2/5/45."

---. "Note de reinsegnements 4/2/45."

---. "Marine en Corse Vedettes ennemies 24/4/45."

---. "Marine en Corse Proces-verbal de capture et état descriptif/inventaire 5/5/45."

---. Dossier TT D 196. "*Montcalm*, 2/1/45,"

---. Prot. 99 EMI ORG du 17/3/45.

Fondo Marina della R.S.I., Archivio dell'Ufficio Storico della Marina Militare, Rome. "Unità navali della Marina Repubblicana al 1 febbraio 1945."

---. "Missioni di guerra effettuate dai mezzi d'assalto della Marina Repubblicana, relazione all'11 marzo 1945."

---. "Notizie sull'Antisom della Marina Repubblicana, relazione del 1 giugno 1945."

Kriegstagebuch der Seekriegsleitung (1. Abteilung) 1939-1945, Part A, Vol. 10. Herford- Bonn: Mittler & Sohn, 1989.

Lagevortraege des Oberbefehlshaber der Kriegsmarine vor Hitler 1939-1945. Munich: Lehamanns, 1972.

Ufficio Storico della Marina Militare. La Marina italiana nella Seconda Guerra Mondiale

Volume II: *Navi perdute*. Rome, 1965.

---. Taffrail *Mediterraneo Occidentale*, Ufficio Storico della Marina Militare. Rome, 1956.

United States Navy. World War II Action and Operational Reports, 1941-1947. Commander Motor Torpedo Boat Squadron Twenty-Two. Action Report night of 29/30 June 1944. College Park, MD: Modern Military Records, National Archives and Records Administration.

---. USS *Benson*, 30 September – 2 October 1944.
---. USS *Charles F. Hughes*, 21 August 1944
---. USS *Gleaves*, 1-2 October 1944.
---. USS *Hilary P. Jones*, 21 August 1944.
---. USS *Ludlow*, 13 November - 11 December 1944.
---. USS *Mackenzie*, 21 April 1945.
---. USS *PC 545*, 18 March 1944.
---. USS *PC 621*. 20 February 1944.
---. USS *PC 626*, 14 May 1944; 24 May 1944.
---. USS *PC 627*. 22 February 1944; 14 May 1944.
---. USS *Woolsey*, 20 October – 4 November 1944

Secondary Sources

Badoglio, Pietro. *Italy in the Second World War: Memories and Documents.* Westport, Conn.: Greenwood, 1976.

Bagnasco, Erminio, and Enrico Cernuschi. *Le Navi da Guerra Italiane 1940–1945.* Parma: Ermanno Albertelli, 2003.

Bagnasco, Erminio and Marco Spertini. *I mezzi d'assalto della X^a Flottiglia MAS*, Parma: Albertelli, 1991.

Bandini, Franco. *Vita e morte segreta di Mussolini.* Milan: Mondadori, 1977.

BBC. People's War. www.bbc.co.uk/history /ww2peopleswar/ stories /08/ a2992908.shtml.

Bolla, Luigi. *Perché a Salò*. Milan: Bompiani, 1982.

Bordogna, Mario. *Junio Valerio Borghese e la X Flottiglia MAS*. Milan: Mursia, 1995.

Bragadin, Marc'Antonio. "Ho visto il messaggio del Re a Caviglia," *Epoca*, 15, August 1965.

Borghese, J. Valerio, trans James Cleugh. *Sea Devils: Italian Navy Commandos in World War II.* Annapolis: Naval Institute Press, 1995.

Bulkley, Robert J. *At Close Quarters: PT Boats in the United States Navy*. Annapolis: Naval Institute Press, 2003.

Canosa, Romano, *L'epurazione in Italia*. Milan: Baldini e Castoldi, 1999.

Carré, Paul. *Le Fantasque: L'odyssée de la 10ᵉ DCL*. Nantes: Marines edition, 1994.

Cernuschi, Enrico, "La Marina Repubblicana 1943-1945." *Storia Militare* (188) May 2009, 41-51 and (189) June 2009, 51-62.

Cernuschi, Enrico and Vincent P. O'Hara. "Mas Contro Destroyers." *Storia Militare* (213). June 2011, 16-26.

Cherpak, Evelyn, ed., *The Memoirs of Admiral H. Kent Hewitt*. Newport, R.I.: Naval War College Press, 2004.

Darrieus, Henri and Jean Quéguiner. *Historique de la Marine française (Novembre 1942 – Août 1945)*. Saint Malo: L'Ancre de Marine, 1994.

Faggioni, Gabriele, "La guerra aeronavale tra il golfo di Venezia e la costa Dalmata dopo l'8 settembre 1943." *Bollettino d'Archivio dell'ufficio storico della Marina Militare*. XXVII, December 2013. 71-127

Festorazzi, Roberto "Führer, liquidiamo il capitolo Russia", *Il Giornale*, 20 July 2001.

Gatti, Carlo. *Il Tigullio un golfo di eroi*. Rapallo, Italy: Busco, 2002.

Green, Jack and Alessandro Massignani. *The Black Prince and the Sea Devils: The Story of Valerio Borghese and the Elite Units of the Decima MAS*. Cambridge, Mass.: Da Capo, 2004.

Hervieux, Pierre. "German TA Torpedo Boats at War." *Warship 1997-1998*. London: Conway, 1997.

Monelli, Paolo. *Roma 1943*. Rome: Migliaresi editore, 1945.

Morison, Samuel Eliot *The Invasion of France and Germany 1944-1945*. Boston: Little Brown, 1974.

---. Sicily – Salerno – Anzio January 1943 – June 1944. Boston: Little Brown, 1990.

Möllhausen, Eitel Friedrich. *La carta perdente, memorie diplomatiche 25 luglio 1943 – 2 maggio 1945*. Rome: Sestante, 1948

Nelson, Curtis L. *Hunters in the Shallows, a History of the PT Boat*. Washington, D.C.: Brassey's, 1998.

Nesi, Sergio, *Decima Flottiglia nostra*. Milan: Mursia, 1986.

---. "Chiaro di luna ad Anzio." *Storia Militare* (142). July 2005.

O'Hara, Vincent P. "Risk vs. Reward off the Italian Rivera." *Naval History* 27(5). October 2013, 56-61.

---. *Struggle for the Middle Sea: The Great Navies at War in the Mediterranean Theater, 1940-1945*. Annapolis: Naval Institute Press, 2009.

O'Hara, Vincent P. and Enrico Cernuschi. *Dark Navy: the Regia Marina and the Armistice of 8 September 1943*. Ann Arbor, Mich.: Nimble, 2009.

O'Reilly, Charles T, *Forgotten Battles: Italy's war of liberation*. Lanham, MD: Lexington Books, 2001, 65.

Pope, Dudley, Flag 4: The Battle of Coastal Forces in the Mediterranean 1939-1945. London: Chatham Publishing, 1998.

Reynolds, Leonard C. *Dog Boats at War: Royal Navy D Class MTBs and MGBs 1939-1945*. Phoenix Mill, England: Sutton, 2000.

---. *Motor Gunboat 658: The Small Boat War in the Mediterranean*. London: Cassell, 2002.

Saibene, Marc. *Les torpilleurs de 1500 tonnes du type* Bourrasque. Nantes: Marines editions, 2001.

Santoni, Alberto. "Doveva consegnarsi al nemico nei porti della Cirenaica Libera." *Storia Illustrata*, August 1982.

Santoni, Alberto and Francesco Mattesini. *La partecipazione tedesca alla guerra aeronavale nel Mediterrananeo (1940-1945)*. Parma: Albertelli, 2005.

Tarchi, Angelo. *Teste Dure*. Milan: S.E.L.C., 1967.

Tomblin, Barbara Brooks. *With Utmost Spirit: Allied Naval Operations in the Mediterranean, 1942-1945*. Lexington, Ky.: The University Press of Kentucky, 2004.

Weichold, Eberhard. "Il contributo della Marina germanica alla guerra nel Mediterraneo," *Il mare*, October, 1959.

Whitley, M. J. *German Coastal Forces of World War Two*. London: Arms and Armour Press, London, 1993.

About the Authors

Vincent P. O'Hara of Chula Vista, California USA and Enrico Cernuschi of Pavia Italy are the authors of *Dark Navy: the Regia Marina and the Armistice of 8 September 1943*. They have collaborated for more than a decade specializing in the Mediterranean during the Second World War. Their work has appeared in the annuals *Warship* and *Seaforth Naval Review* as well as publications including *Naval War College Review*, *Storia Militare*, *World War II*, *World War II History*, and *World War II Quarterly*.

Books by Enrico Cernuschi

Marinelettro e il radiotelemetro italiano (1995)
La notte del Lupo (1997)
I sette minuti di Punta Stilo (1998)
Il sottomarino italiano (1999)
Domenico Cavagnari, Storia di un ammiraglio (2001)
Fuoco dal mare (2002)
Le navi da guerra italiane, (2003) with Erminio Bagnasco
Vincere, vinceremo…e se avessimo vinto? (2005)
Contro amici e nemici, la guerra fredda della Marina Militare, 1947-1979 (2005)
La vittoria in prestito (2006)
Fecero tutti il loro dovere (2006)
La Marina italiana nella Seconda guerra mondiale, una bibliografia critica (2010)
Le Navi Ospedale italiane 1935-1945 (2010) with Erminio Bagnasco and Maurizio Brescia
Gran Pavese Storie di mare, di guerra e di fiume (2011)
Navi e Quattrini (2013)
ULTRA. La fine di un mito. La guerra dei codici tra gli inglesi e le Marine italiane 1934-1945 (2014)
Battaglie sconosciute: Storia della Regia Marina durante la Grande Guerra (2014)

Books by Vincent P. O'Hara

German Fleet at War (2004)
The U.S. Navy against the Axis (2007)
Struggle for the Middle Sea (2009)
On Seas Contested (2010) editor with David Dickson and Richard Worth
In Passage Perilous (2012)
The Royal Navy's Revenge (2012)
To Crown the Waves (2013) editor with David Dickson and Richard Worth

www.ingramcontent.com/pod-product-compliance
Lightning Source LLC
Chambersburg PA
CBHW042337150426
43195CB00001B/15